Silent Songs
of
Worship

God's Tabernacle Within Us

D1082397

by

Terri L. Terry

Dedication

To my mother, my friend.
Her life in the wilderness silently sang Jesus to me.

Acknowledgments

My deepest gratitude goes to:

LIZA TERRY, my daughter, who has danced through the wilderness with me;

JUDSON CORNWALL, who believed in this book;

SUSAN HOSMER, for her immovable friendship;

SAM SASSER, whose life shouted of Jesus;

FLO SASSER, who is a fountain of prayer;

TOM TERRY, who taught me many things;

KIT NEWLIN, for her encouragement;

SAM AND PAULETTE FARINA, who poured their lives into me;

DARYL AND BARBARA SANDERS, who helped me grow as a minister;

RON COTTLE, who gave me the opportunity to teach;

JESUS, MY LORD, who has taught me to listen for His silent songs.

Contents

Foreword

The subject of worship is now more popular than ever. New books on worship are released regularly, CDs and videos introduce new sounds in worship, and many churches have more persons involved in the worship arm of activities than in anything else.

We who are deeply involved in teaching, leading and practicing worship are used to going to the Old Testament's Tabernacle in the wilderness for a pattern of worship. It is a legitimate and practical quest, for God Himself gave Israel both the methods and the means for worship in that place. Therefore, we should never ignore the Tabernacle.

For many years I taught on the Tabernacle. I even built a scale model of the edifice to help students visualize its structure. My second book, *Let Us Draw Near*, was about the Tabernacle and what it symbolizes to us today.

When I was given a copy of the manuscript for Terri L. Terry's book, *Silent Songs of Worship: God's Tabernacle Within Us*, I purposed to briefly scan it. However, after reading a page or two, I was so captivated by the style of writing, the progression of concepts and the fundamental truths that I read the entire book.

Silent Songs of Worship uses the Tabernacle as a framework, but it is not an exposition of the sacred tent alone. This book is concerned with the process that God uses to make worshipers of us all.

I wish that the U.S. Congress would pass a law requiring all worship leaders, singers and musicians to read this book. Written by a professional musician, it explores the worship of the human spirit and extols this as greater than the mere musical expression of the soul.

This book does not condemn; it challenges. It reveals to us a higher, *"more excellent way."* It does warn us, however: "Expecting God's presence because we have performed the ritual is not worship. Rather, it smacks of incantation."

For all who sincerely desire to become worshipers, not merely musicians and singers, the principles Terri L. Terry expounds in this work will be invaluable. It reads easily, but it will apply painfully. The end product will be something that is sorely lacking in most worship conferences and churches—*pure worship.*

Judson Cornwall
Phoenix, Arizona

Introduction

Why this book? What is its purpose? The answer can probably be found in the years that I have served as pastor, Bible teacher and worship leader.

For several years prior to beginning this text, I had experienced an inward "wince" over the pride that I saw in myself as a trained musician and worship leader. My interior pain was exacerbated each time I descended from a church platform to the words of some well-meaning saint who told me, "Oh, Terri, the worship was just wonderful this morning!" Mind you, as a musician, those words massaged my ego. Yet my spirit chafed, and I wasn't quite sure why. Why did this sweet saint believe that *my* performance of *music* was *her* experience of *worship*?

Just about the time that I began to be able to verbalize my interior discomfort, I was assigned to teach a class on Moses' Tabernacle at a Bible college where I was on staff. Because of my extensive musical background, I honestly thought that I was fairly well prepared for another study in worship. Nothing could have been further from the truth.

In my preparation to teach Moses' Tabernacle, I began to perceive *God's* idea of worship. To my chagrin, I found that worship from God's perspective has nothing to do with musical excellence. Though all my previous studies of David's Tabernacle had emphasized the importance of music, I discovered that God's ultimate intention for worship has little to do with audible music at all.

God's intention, I discovered, is to create the music of His presence *within* us. Greater than mere musical expression of the soul, God wants you and me, the Tabernacle of His habitation, to reverberate with His *inaudible* music. As I studied the types and symbols of Moses' Tabernacle, every piece of Tabernacle furniture, each material used in the building of the Tabernacle, even the wilderness itself in which it existed became an integral part of a new kind of music. I began to hear *new* songs, *silent songs.* Though previously I had always been the "composer" of my own worship expression to God, I was awestruck to discover that this "absent-of-noise" music being written within me was both *from* God and *to* God.

There may be those who are satisfied with merely audible music as an expression of worship. I, for one, am not, and this book is my response. I want to learn every silent note that Jesus creates as He tabernacles within me. I trust that you do too.

Terri L. Terry
Fortson, Georgia

Chapter One

The Silent Song

"Be still, and know that I am God."
(Psalm 46:10)

A silent song? Isn't that an oxymoron? How can there be music or singing without sound? Is there such a thing as a silent song? If so, where in the universe would it be heard?

Such a wild supposition must seem absurd. To talk of worship these days without talking of singing and music must sound ludicrous to the average worshiper. After all, the past years of instruction at worship conferences have made music the centrality of worship. But to me, that fact is frightening.

Please understand, dear worshipers, "I am one of you!" I am a musician, graduated from a respected conservatory with two music degrees. I have been a music educator for over thirty years and have recorded and played professionally. I truly love music. And I love worshiping Jesus through music. But something is wrong.

There is a trend that disturbs me deeply. We singers and musicians often revel in the effect that worship music has on us. We enjoy hearing ourselves worship. The experience of singing and playing for Jesus has become something of a spiritual drug for us. It dizzies us.

Never mind that "excellence in the arts" has taken precedence over pastoring God's people. Never mind that most small churches can in no way master the intricate rhythms and harmonies of many choruses being written today. Never mind that the songs we embrace today are profuse with the words *me, mine* and *our*.

Have we exchanged God's intention for the complexity of musicianship? Are we singing the latest chorus in our services only because the worship team feels bored or musically unchallenged? Are we, as musicians, merely displaying our gifts and anointings? Are today's churches filled with musical excellence without being filled with an excellence of spirit? Sometimes, I fear, the answer is yes.

We musicians intimately know our craft. We know rhythms and notes. But do we know the Lord's silent songs? Can we all be honest enough to declare that we find ourselves in a kind of spiritual cul-de-sac, circling round and round? Are we trying to convince everyone, including ourselves, that this musical merry-go-round is God's intention for worship?

I want to abandon the cul-de-sac. How about you? Let us rise and follow our Lord, for I believe that He is drawing us out.

God is waiting in the wilderness to teach us His new songs, *silent songs* of surrender and sacrifice, gratitude and giving, faith and fellowship. These inaudible songs are music to His ears.

A Prayer for Silent Music

Lord, my ears are full of my own song.
Please silence the fortissimo of me, myself *and* I
in my worship.
The music that I desperately need to hear is the
still, small Voice that quietly sings within me.

I know about outward silence.
Now teach me to know inward silence, a silence
that is filled with Your music.
I don't want to miss a single note.

So, draw me near.

Chapter Two

The Conservatory
of Interior Worship

"...Christ in you, the hope of glory."
(Colossians 1:27)

*A*ll would-be singers and musicians must undergo training. They must learn music from the inside out. Rudimentary skills must be inlaid into the mosaic of their musicianship. The monotony of honing and polishing scales, harmony and intonation must be endured before there can be any visible evidence of the artistry they desire.

All of the required skills will be learned because of a performer's hunger to express his or her love of music. So, the budding musician willingly enters a place of intensive study — the conservatory.

Upon his arrival at the conservatory, the young musician is often stunned to realize that he is not assigned exciting hours upon the sprawling stage to display his gift. Instead, his schedule of studies has him buried for endless hours in a small room in the basement of the conservatory — the practice room.

Often no larger than a closet, this tiny room will be the Bethlehem of the musician's artistry. He will practice alone, and he will practice constantly. Repetition will lead to more repetition. Silently and unnoticed he will file away at the steel girders that imprison his musicianship. Then, like a butterfly released from its wormy cocoon, his skills will finally be released on the wings of mature artistry. With each seemingly mundane practice hour, his obedience becomes art.

All of the necessary techniques of skillful musicianship are mastered in a conservatory designed to channel and shape the young musician's passion. And it is no different for those who would sing *silent songs*. If we are to learn to worship *"in spirit and in truth,"* we cannot begin on a large church platform. We must go and study in the conservatory of worship that God, the Great Composer, has provided — the Tabernacle.

The Tabernacle was established in Heaven before the foundations of the world, but it was first seen by men's eyes in the dusty wilderness of Sinai. Years later, the Father clothed the Tabernacle in flesh. His name was Jesus. He silently sang among us. Now, God's intention is that the Tabernacle of Worship be revealed within *you*.

Will you enter and learn of Jesus' silent music? Yes? Then from now on I will address you as *"Singer."*

A Prayer Within the Conservatory

*Lord, grace me to learn of Your music within me.
Help me to recognize that You* are *singing
within me.*

*Assign me those scales and rudiments of life that
can file away at the steel girders of myself.
They imprison Your songs.*

*And Lord, help me not to care how long it takes.
I want to be known as a singer of* silent songs.

Draw me nearer.

Chapter Three

The Song of the Wilderness

"Let my people go, so they can worship me in the wilderness."
(Exodus 7:16, NLT)

*W*here would this tabernacle of *silent songs* be located? Would it be constructed in a bustling city or perhaps near a gentle brook? Would it be shaded by a cool, green forest? Where would God choose to build His place of worship? Surprisingly, God's choice was the desert — the wilderness.

The wilderness was the perfect place for those who desired to deepen their love of the Lord to learn *silent songs* of worship. So, going into the wilderness was part of God's plan for them. Moses led the children Israel out of slavery and into an arid wasteland for one purpose and one purpose alone — and that was to worship God.

> *Let my people go, so that they may worship me in*
> *the desert.*   Exodus 7:16, NIV

Anyone who hungers after silent music will journey into the sandy places. This includes you. The wilderness is a brutal, yet perfect, schoolmaster. But Jesus wants you to learn something there. He wants you to learn to *lean* on Him

But you might ask, "Why the wilderness? It is a dry, violently hot, drab, uninhabited, lonely place

that seems to shout desolation. It frightens me."
Yes, I have heard that being in the wilderness feels
like a dark night with no hope of light. A friend
who was there says that being in the wilderness
gives one the sense of sleep with no hope of
awakening. (Now, surprisingly, she says that she
wouldn't trade the experience for anything.)

But having to go to such a place doesn't make
sense. This woman is a good Christian. Why would
God take her into the desert? Why would God take
me into the desert? *And if God takes me into the wilderness, will He abandon me there?* you may be
thinking.

No, you will not be abandoned. You will be
groomed to sing *silent songs.*

Worship has, for too long, been a vehicle that the
church has used for its own pleasure. Expecting to
experience God's presence because we have performed the ritual is not worship. Rather, it
smacks of incantation.

God's way of birthing His silent music within us
is far more intricate than we have been taught. His
work in a seeker is mostly invisible. His deepest
transformations will not always be done in an ex-
pansive, crowded auditorium. No, more often than
not, His tool of choice is the severe efficiency of the
desert.

The wilderness is mentioned more than three
hundred times throughout the Scriptures. The

Hebrew word for wilderness includes the following meanings: "a sense of driving; an open field; a pasture." God's purpose for this wilderness journey is not to punish you or limit you, but to birth in you His silent music. Without the mercy of the wilderness, you will forever remain untouched by Him. In the desert of your days, you can learn to become deaf to the voice of your own selfish love songs: self-songs that bargain with God, self-songs that endlessly whine, self-songs that refuse to surrender.

Only in the wilderness can Jesus teach you how to stop whining about everything and everyone. Only in the wilderness can your childish caterwauling be conquered. Only in the wilderness can you learn not to live for yourself. And so He *purposefully* brings you into the wilderness.

In Old Testament times, the wilderness was the place where kings warred. Is it so different for you and me? A thirsty throat and parched skin force a believer into battle. But the war to be waged in the wilderness is not against principalities in high places. Rather, the carnage of this battle will be inflicted on self — self-pity, self-centeredness, self-sufficiency, self-indulgence and self-love. It is in this war that the sharp tongue, the harsh hand and the proud heart will be dealt a deathblow. Slowly, and only in God's timing, the desert will enable you to learn that the poison of self is drained out one drop at a time — and only in the wilderness.

Interestingly enough, in Hebrew, the name for the Wilderness of Paran means *beauty*. God's Word declares:

> *Precious in the sight of the Lord is the death of his saints.*   Psalm 116:15

Could it be that in the eyes of our Lord, the sight of our not being so taken up with ourselves is quite beautiful to Him? This and, oh, so much more awaits you in the wilderness. Welcome it, Singer.

Spewed out of the mouth of Pharaoh, the people of Israel were thrust into the wilderness. Having prevailed only through God's awesome displays of power and with the taste of the lamb still in their mouths, they lifted their gaze toward the desert. By the strength of the Lord's right arm, they had been released from bondage. They moved out gladly into that barren, rocky terrain. Why did they want to go? God had drawn them out to worship.

You and I are no different. At an altar of release, in the midst of a divine encounter, we gladly acquiesce to Him. We will do all that He asks. With the sweetness of His presence upon our tongues, we covenant anew.

Be sure, Singer, that He has heard your vow of surrender, and He will set in motion the mechanics to extract precisely what you surrendered at that altar. For you, like Israel, were redeemed for one purpose — to worship Him:

And God said, "I will be with you. And this will be the sign to you that it is I who have sent you: When you have brought the people out of Egypt, you will worship God on this mountain."

Exodus 3:12

So, now He calls you into the wilderness, not to stifle you, but to sing His character into you. All whose hearts are continually drawn into deeper knowledge of the Father are invited into the desert's diminuendo of self. He must increase, and you must decrease.

Will you go through the wilderness after Him? I think you will. By God's grace and your choice, you will go. You will go, even into the desert. You cannot bear the alternative. You cannot bear to deny Him, for He is your Beloved.

Yours is the cry of the lovesick. You are beginning to follow hard after your Lord. His music, in difficult as well as gentle winds, is beginning to flow through you. Are you willing to search anywhere, even the wilderness, to learn His *silent songs*? As Solomon so eloquently wrote:

By night on my bed I sought him whom my soul loveth: I sought him, but I found him not. I will rise now, and go about the city in the streets, and in the broad ways I will seek him whom my soul loveth. Song of Solomon 3:1-2, KJV

Do Jeremiah's words describe your own fervor?

*Go and proclaim in the hearing of Jerusalem,
Thus says the LORD: I remember the devotion of
your youth, your love as a bride, how you followed me in the wilderness in a land not sown.*

Jeremiah 2:2, NRS

Have you tasted and seen how good He is? Are
you hungry to be wholly His? If so, you will go.

With that decision, you will, like all of God's
worshipers, find yourself, after many days' journey
in the scorching sun, waiting at the base of Mount
Sinai. Waiting ... A wilderness experience always
includes waiting.

The people of Israel had to wait, too. They stood
restlessly at the base of this same mountain. And
while they chafed at the base of the mountain,
Moses, their leader, ascended the heights and drew
near to the Lord, who had descended upon the
mountain of fire. The smoke from the fire covered
the mountain of God's presence. And, with this, a
sense of awe filled this desert.

Then God spoke. Listen to His words. He said,
"You were redeemed for worship, and worship is
an interior relationship with Me. You shall have no
other gods before Me. Our intimate relationship
will preclude all others. Out of our silent worship
duet will flow every song of charity to the world."

Because of these words, the people of Israel began to realize why they had been delivered into the desert. But how could they express this relationship? Where would they meet with God to learn the intimate music silently sung between Creator and creature? God would build His tent among them, and there He would teach them.

God had seen far beyond everything the callow spiritual eyes of the Israelites could grasp, and His desire to meet with them was far greater than their infant devotion. The Infinite One, the One who reigns in and beyond eternity (for He has even created eternity itself), would teach His people His own *silent songs.*

Gazing backward, far into the realm of eternity, God saw the slain Lamb. Before Him, He saw the Bride, the wife. Then, with infinite patience and intricate detail, He envisioned the perfect place of encounter — a tabernacle in the wilderness, His conservatory of worship, a holy edifice to house *silent songs*. This structure would accommodate the exquisite intimacies of divine marriage.

Knowing the undeniable dullness of ears that long to hear the silent whisper of His voice, the Lord tenderly imparts, in shadows, the realities of the splendors of worship-relationship available to those marked as His. Altars, bloody sacrifices, precious metals and obedience will create a tent of relationship *IN THE WILDERNESS.*

Having been instructed by God to do so, the Israelites began the daunting task of building a replica
of Heaven's Tabernacle. In eternity, the Father's
House has been erected on the pure silver girders
of the Lamb's blood since before the foundation of
the world. But now, an earthly model would be
built.

Thousands of years ago, that first Tabernacle of
worship appeared in the Sinai desert. Then, the living Tabernacle of worship sang among us as the
Father's only Son. Now, His silent music is to be
composed within you.

What would the Tabernacle be like? For one
thing, it would have no floor. Those who wor-
shiped in it would forever carry the dust of earth
upon their feet. It would be a tent, streamlined and
highly portable. It would be small. Two tiny rooms
and a modest yard would house every imaginable
aspect of worship. There would be an open Outer
Court, a covered Holy Place, and a most sacred secret chamber known as the Most Holy Place. Each
part of this trinity of compartments would contain
unique and specific instruments of worship.

The yard, or courtyard, would hold a huge
bronze-covered altar from which the pungent aroma
of sacrifice would never cease to rise. Adjacent to
this altar of blood would stand a large bronze basin.
The water within this laver would shimmer in the
light of the burning coals of sacrifice.

The Holy Place would be covered with four heavy layers of curtains and animal skins. Beneath these soft ceilings, a majestic golden lampstand would illuminate the golden walls of the room. From another altar, the sweet fragrance of holy incense would fill the nostrils of both God and man. At a small golden table, God's eyes would feast on the bread that would continually be placed before His face.

Beyond a heavy and exquisite veil would lie the most intimate chamber—the Holy of Holies. The only object within this tiny room would be a divine ark. The cherubim that rose out of the ends of this most holy of objects would fix their gaze upon the very heart of God.

Within this secret place ... God Himself would sing. And He has ordained that you hear His silent music. Where? In the wilderness.

A Prayer in the Wilderness

Lord, as I take my first faltering steps into the sand, I hear Your song calling me.
I wish I could rejoice or shout, or be boldly courageous.
But I cannot.

There is no bravado here.
I am frightened by the wilderness.
What will I lose?

Yet I am more frightened by my future if I do not follow You.
Still, I would rather lose me than You.

Help me, Lord.
Don't let anything turn me back.

And when my days are accomplished, cause me to come up from the wilderness singing with You.

Jesus, draw me nearer.

Chapter Four

The Song of the Linen Wall

"And he made the court...of fine twined linen."
(Exodus 38:9, KJV)

*Y*es, God is singing His song of love to you from within the desert. This most profound music will be written within your own secret place. To learn the first notes of His silent symphony, you must first encounter a partition. What sort of partition is it? It is a *linen wall*.

Singer, I see you standing, gazing with your heart turned toward the Holy of Holies. Are you listening to this incredible *silent song*? Are you yearning for the same sweet music to be composed somehow within your own life? If only you could see the Source.

But your view of the Source of that music is blocked. That song of songs ... where is it coming from? That exquisite melody ... who is singing it? You cannot know the answer outside of the Courtyard. You cannot see over the barrier of the soft linen curtain-wall.

Enclosing the Tabernacle was a white linen wall. This fence of linen, which enclosed an area of approximately fifty yards by twenty-five yards, was God's barrier of choice. No one could draw near to the divine music without first learning the song of this linen fence.

I hear your question: "Why would God open the Red Sea to His children and then cordon off His courts of worship? They had followed Him into the wilderness, hadn't they? What was He trying to show them? Couldn't they just worship where they were?"

Of course they could, and so can you. You can stop right here. But Jesus' silent music is so captivating, so compelling. Will you allow Him to draw you even nearer? If your answer is yes, He will teach you the song of the linen wall. You see, beloved Singer, He wants you to become a virtuoso of many *silent songs*. This is His next lesson. So, come, let us find out why He has enclosed the Tabernacle with a linen wall. Why is there a barrier to worship?

It is because God has given all things boundaries. Think about it: Oceans have shores, stars stay in the heavens and so forth. In the same way, worship-relationship has God-ordained boundaries.

This linen wall divides, and in the wilderness you must face it and, yes, even embrace, it.

Worship also divides. It separates spectators from participants and voyeurs from lovers. Singer, the journey from observation to intimacy begins at the linen fence. But will you come? He is drawing you.

Why linen? Why not cotton or wool? But no other fabric was used in the Tabernacle — only linen. God used this fabric *exclusively* to surround and define His courtyard of worship. Linen has a lesson for us. What will we learn from this common cloth? We will learn linen's song of surrender.

Linen comes from the flax plant, which is said to be a woody plant. In the Scriptures, wood symbolically speaks of our humanity, of human inability and weakness. Yet God chose the by-products of woody flax to create beautiful white linen.

The process by which the woody flax is transformed into linen is complex. Moving from splinters to splendor is excruciating. Nonetheless, like the flax plant, you and I must surrender to this process if we are to become a part of the Tabernacle's songs.

Grown to the height of approximately six feet, flax is selected by the miller for use while it is in full bloom. Bundles of this plant are gathered only at the appropriate time and season. (Be assured, Singer, that on your journey toward the Source of your song, Jesus will carefully watch until He has sufficiently strengthened you to begin the process.)

Once the time of harvest has begun, the bundled stalks of flax are immediately submerged in deep pools of water. Here they must soak for a long time. You see, buried within all that woodiness, there lies a single precious fiber. It lies deep inside the core of each stalk, and it must be freed, or released. Within this hidden core is the very essence of the white linen.

To become able to sing linen's melody, you will have to soak. You will have to become willing to be submerged. At various times in your life, the sub-aqueous atmosphere of obedience to God will have to become your entire world. It will have to become your very life and breath.

It may seem unbelievable, but you have been brought into the dry, thirsty desert to become satu-rated, wet clear through, saturated in Jesus. By drowning in Him, the woody humanity that you are bound in will eventually decompose. Then, and only then, the water of His liquid love will make its way into your awaiting heart and begin to free it to silently sing.

Jesus knew this immersion. Have you ever con-sidered that the Father could have released Jesus into His public ministry much sooner? Why not send the Savior as a full-grown man to the earth? Why not let Jesus just appear as a mature indi-vidual and reveal the love of His Father?

But no, the Father, in His wise mercy, held His Son beneath the surface for thirty obscure years. Though Christ had known His Father intimately as the royal Son, still, as a Man in the wilderness of the earth, Jesus had something yet to learn. He had to learn obedience. He had to learn obedience at the hands of an ordinary carpenter and his wife.

Jesus allowed Himself to be submerged in the water of submissiveness to the clumsy clay of that divinely chosen couple. He did this as worship. He learned, in a very practical and real way, that obedience *always* precedes sacrifice.

Jesus' desire was to become *surrendered linen* for His Father's Tabernacle. His cry was to lovingly sing that *silent song*, and it will be the same for you.

Still, much more processing of the flax is needed. When the Miller sees that the core strand of the flax has finally been exposed by its watery baptism, He proceeds. By this time, the wood of the plant has begun to rot.

Now He places the infant fiber under even greater stress. Limp from the water, the would-be linen fibers are subjected to seemingly greater humiliations. First, they are placed beneath grooved rollers to break them. Then, sharp razors are used to cut them. This process is known as "whipping."

Next, an iron comb is applied to stroke the fibers, to further separate them for their intended use. This combing, known as "heckling," is the final process that the Miller uses to insure the finest material.

If the linen is to become beautiful and long-lasting, able to sing in the wind, these seemingly cruel processes are necessary and glorious tools in the Miller's hands. Having been lovingly subjected to these essential processes, the flax fiber becomes yielded to the Weaver's intention for it.

Then, at last, it is fit for the Tabernacle. It has been transformed into a fabric for worship.

As you journey into the wilderness to learn the *silent songs* of worship, Jesus will call you to become many things. But first, He calls you to become linen. He draws you to become the workmanship of His hands, the fabric of obedience and submission to Him.

Oh, Singer, allow God, through your wilderness experience, to make you linen. Embrace this time of being submerged. God is behind all things. Learn to look up through the overwhelming, murky waters and see Him governing it all. Your obedient submission to the submersion will separate you for the Tabernacle. It will become the elementary notes of obedience for your Father who is listening for your first *silent song.*

A Prayer at the Linen Wall

Lord, I am very much flax.
I'm entangled in my own humanity, for I still
want so much of this world.
Therefore, I need the difficult things You allow.

Submerge me as You will, for as long as You will,
that I might learn obedience, that I might learn
surrender, that I might become linen for Your
courts, able to easily flow and sing in the wind of
Your Spirit.

Then, draw me nearer.

Chapter Five

The Song of the Colorful Gate

*"And the hanging for the gate of the court
was needlework, of blue, and purple,
and scarlet, and fine twined linen."*
(Exodus 38:18, KJV)

*W*ithin the circumference of the pristine white linen wall, there was an opening. This opening had been produced by obedience and submission. The yielded flax now lay within the Weaver's hands, and the first notes of *silent music* were being sung. It was God Himself who had begun it.

Through the seemingly brutal surroundings of the wilderness, God has composed the initial notes of His symphony within you. Your cry to know Him, even in the wilderness, is being answered. Now, He desires to draw you through the *gate* that is open before you.

This gate is the *only* entrance to the courts of the Lord. It is the only access to the interior of the Tabernacle. Many people desire silent worship and enter singing the sacrifice of praise. But remember, sacrifice is always preceded by obedience.

Abraham had to obey the Lord before he even approached Mount Moriah. He had to first obediently get up, take his servants and his son with him, and prepare the firewood for the altar. His heart had to obey first, and then, and only then, could he proceed with the actual sacrifice.

Now consider Cain. Cain tried to initiate his own method of worship. He foolishly thought that he could circumvent obedience and submission.

Saul did the same thing. Thinking to impress man and God (though mostly himself), he would not yield to obedience. He was sure his sacrifice would supersede specific orders from God. But silent music can only be sung by humbled hearts. If humility is shunned, violence will flourish. Without the humility of obedience, worship itself will become the goal.

Music for music's sake, worship for worship's sake, ministry for ministry's sake ... this is how the Kingdom suffers the violence of disobedience. Worship without humility becomes a place to take and not to give, a time to force my own way rather than allowing God to have His way.

Today, sadly, many follow Cain and Saul, believing that mere singing, without obedience, affords them access to the court. But not you. You are learning.

The gate stood on the east side of the linen wall, near the tribe of Judah. Is that significant? Yes, it is. The east is the direction from which things *open*. From the east, the sun daily initiates a new day. It is the eastern sky that will split to mark the return of Jesus for His people. And the tribe of Judah, whose name means "praise," will hallow and hedge the opening in the linen wall. The gate is the birthplace of praise to God.

The Song of the Colorful Gate

The song of the gate will be learned in the east. Having submitted to the lesson of the song of the linen wall, you have opened yourself to new melodies—the four refrains of the eastern gate. Each song will be learned by understanding the colors God had embroidered into it: blue, purple, scarlet and white.

Though the linen fence was mostly solid white, the gate of the Tabernacle was a quartet of colors singing a unique melody, each hue having a distinct lyric. Yet their intertwined theme remained constant: praise at *all* times. God requires praise through your blue days, as well as through your days of victory. He requires praise while you bleed and praise for the work God is accomplishing in your life.

At the gate, your interior themes will learn to harmonize with Jesus' life of praise. Your life will start to resound with His artistry. The four hues, or colors, of the gate must be carefully woven into the fibers of your life. At the gate, your heart is to be placed upon the Weaver's loom so that He can embroider it with each of these four brave and beautiful stains. It will be a stunning masterpiece, the joy of the Artist.

And the hanging for the gate of the court was needlework, of blue, and purple, and scarlet, and fine twined linen.　　　Exodus 38:18, KJV

What does each of these colors signify? Let us see.

Blue

Blue was the first color, and blue must always be first, for it is the symbol of God in His Heaven. He is always preeminent. He is Initiator and Creator. Worship-relationship was His thought. A Tabernacle of Worship built within us was *His* idea. We love and worship Him *only* because He first loved us.

Blue is a symbol of God's choice to initiate grace toward us. As bankrupt paupers, we could only wait for the Father to deposit the treasure of His Son's music within us. In His amazing love, He launched an arrow of divine grace into our dull hearts. And by doing so, God has enabled us to worship Him.

Just what does this grace mean to you? It means dependence on God. It means letting God do in you what you cannot do in yourself. You can't live the Christian life; only Jesus can. So, it means drawing on His faith, as He drew on the faith of His Father. Just as Jesus relied on His Father for every note of Calvary's song, you must trust Jesus for your silent music.

The blue threads of the gate sing the song of childlike trust in God's grace. Praise God for it.

The Song of the Colorful Gate
Purple

The next color embroidered into the praise song of the gate was purple, and purple speaks of royalty. Matthew's gospel portrays Jesus as King of kings. And He has marked us as a nation of kings, destined to rule and reign.

You are a child of the King. The purple fibers of the gate declare it. But do you know over whom you are to be a king? Who exactly is the subject of your royal authority?

You are to be king over an old man. Who is this old man and what is he like? He is an "acquirer." He always wants. How did he get that way? Once, a very long time ago, he chose to ignore God's warnings against partaking of a food that would change him. Now, this old man is addicted to that enticing fruit of avarice and is regularly intoxicated with its wine. This choice forever changed him into a "taker."

The most frightening thing about his addiction, however, is that he can hide it. When he is filled with the fermented wine of "taking," this old man is cunningly adept at cloaking himself in religious acts. Quite convincingly, he declares what is good or bad in all matters related to worship. A frightful dementia has reduced his thought processes to a stringent adjerence to dogma. In the deep recesses of his soul he secretly entertains the thought that worship is really *for his own pleasure*.

He is deaf to the relentless din of his twisted judgments. He pronounces them as music to the ears of God. Bursting with pride and false humility, he outwardly sings praises to the Lord. Inwardly, however, he sings of himself.

Though his lips brim with Christian buzzwords, worship choruses and new revelations, his behavior eventually betrays his true loyalty—*personal promotion*. Generally, he is irritable with anyone who doesn't agree with his opinions. He wags his finger and scoffs at the simplicity of a silent singer.

Oh, and yes, he doesn't mind showing anyone how very gifted, intelligent or talented he is. Do you recognize this old man? Are you brave enough to admit that he lives in you? *He* is the one over whom you are to reign.

You have the power, through the royalty of Jesus, to silence this old man. And you must do just that — through the power of the King of kings within you. Silence him.

In fact, you can learn no more strains of inaudible music until you begin to do this. Remember the azure-blue grace of God that sings within you. Trust God's grace to close the old man's mouth. Let God do in you what you cannot do in yourself.

Allow the new man to sing, and praise God for *His* royal voice.

Scarlet is the third color that painted the entrance. Scarlet is the color of arterial blood that has been spilled in service. Mark's gospel paints Jesus as the suffering servant:

> *For even the Son of man came not to be ministered unto, but to minister, and to give his life a ransom for many.*   Mark 10:45, KJV

Singer, you will be allowed the privilege of serving and suffering alongside your Savior. The scarlet threads of the gate ordain it. Suffering is the womb of a child called worship.

Have you suffered? Have you been scraped or bruised by others? Have you been allowed the mercy of a piercing thorn? If you have, your bleeding wounds will supply the scarlet stain necessary to weave another melody into God's gate of praise. You see, Singer, entering into the fellowship of His sufferings is a narrow door to an intimate knowledge of Jesus.

Singer, I think that you probably already know this truth: If you have followed His voice into the wilderness to learn *silent songs,* you will rarely be without trials. No doubt, since you've made the decision to be a silent singer, you are having difficulties even now. Does you life seem to be "a mess"? Is everything falling apart around you? Are you starting to know the fellowship of Jesus' sufferings? Jesus' life was filled with humiliations. Beloved child of God, why are you horrified at your own momentary humiliation?

Do not be surprised, dear friends, at the fiery test that is coming upon you, as if you were experiencing something unheard of. Instead, be joyful that you are sharing to some degree the sufferings of Christ, in order that at the revealing of His glory you may be full of joy.

1 Peter 4:12-13, MLB

How will you ever learn Jesus' *silent song* if you don't look for Him where He is to be found — in the symphony of His sufferings?

Silent music is costly, astronomically expensive. The price seems almost unconscionable. Still, the full artistry of the Lord's song within you cannot be sung without the color scarlet.

So, as your precious song of silent praise is being written, please remember that God has allowed all things. He knows exactly how much suffering you will be offered. So praise God for every thorn.

White

Finally, fine white linen was the basic canvas into which these other three colors were embroidered.

Your journey into deep worship-relationship can only be based on the holy work previously accomplished by the Weaver, that of submission. The cloth for the gate is identical to that used in the courtyard wall—woody, human flax that has become prized linen. Praise God for the work He is even now doing in you.

The gate of the Tabernacle is the birthplace of praise *"at all times"*:

> *I will bless the Lord at all times; His praise shall continually be in my mouth.*   Psalm 34:1

Singer, *"at all times"* praise.

A Prayer at the Gate

Help me, Lord!
The gate that You open before me is terrifyingly
beautiful.
Each color that You offer to sing within me stirs
up frightening, yet wonderful, possibilities.

I hesitate here at the opening to Your courts.
But my aspiration for Your silent song *in the*
deepest caverns of my spirit gusts and howls for
more of You.
I can't seem to muzzle it.

So, Lord, color, daub, shadow or shade my life
with the artistry of any circumstance or event
that will paint into my silent music the reality of
Your gate of praise.

I want *to praise you AT ALL TIMES.*

So, draw me nearer still.

Chapter Six

The Song of the Brazen Altar

*"And you shall make an altar of acacia wood
…and you shall overlay it with bronze."*
(Exodus 27:1-2)

*H*aving passed through the gate of praise and entered into the Outer Court, you and I will be confronted immediately by an enormous place of slaughter. The largest instrument of worship within the entire Tabernacle was a mammoth place of death. It was called the *brazen altar*. This altar stood just inside the four-colored gate of praise.

In the Tabernacle of worship that Moses built, there was a continual flow of blood from this huge, fiery intersection. Daily, in this Old Testament prototype, animals were continually slaughtered at this altar. Bulls, lambs and goats were sacrificed there. Then their bodies were set ablaze as an act of worship. Now, you stand before the brazen altar. What *silent song* will you learn here?

There can be no further progress in the silent symphony of God without encountering this crossroads. This is, in fact, another great divide. Within the fire of this holy worship instrument, great treasure is smelted. This is the worship-furnace of God. It is the great concert hall of worship. It is the music of the cross.

Many choose to turn away at this divine intersection. Mind you, this is not the cross of salvation. No, this brazen altar is beyond being brought through the Red Sea of redemption. Rather, this altar represents a decision to go beyond suffering. It represents a decision for death.

This cross divides your will from God's. At this altar, Jesus becomes Lord, not just Savior. Here, you will bend low to embrace your cross. God requires that at the brazen altar you learn a fundamental new song—the song of Calvary. And who is His instructor? It is sacrifice.

Singer, do you truly desire to sing *this* music? Then learn the song of the brazen altar.

Approximately seven and a half feet square and four and a half feet high, this altar was the largest of all the instruments of worship in the Tabernacle of worship. Every other piece of worship furniture could easily fit within it. Yes, this altar-cross and its song of sacrifice is the bedrock for all authentic worship. This melody is for the divine ear alone. The notes mastered at this altar are sung in death — your death.

This is not a physical death, but it is a death nonetheless. And what must die here? What must lie here in the ashes? Animals, beasts — *your* animals, *your* beasts — must die here.

The animals in your life that must be slain upon this altar-cross are your dreams, your ambitions, your abilities, your pleasures. As your beasts lie bleeding and dying upon the brazen altar, a holy chasm within your spirit and soul will be opened to make room for more of the Lord's interior music.

If you study its architecture, you will find that this altar was designed to be hollow within. It is your Father's will that you be emptied of all things. Why? It is so that He might fit you for an ever-growing crescendo of His Kingdom melody within.

Do you really want this song, Singer? If you do, then seek to hold nothing but Christ. For His sake, become empty that He may stretch forth in you. See His hand in all things and in all people. It is God who uses everything to empty you of yourself. That is not the enemy. It is the brazen altar singing. It is the cross of worship.

The world (and yes, even the Church as a whole) might never want to hear this melody, but you are here at this altar seeking its hidden song. Once again, I ask, do you really want *this* song?

Fitted with a horn at each of its four corners, the brazen altar was a place of being *tied down*. At this place, unwilling animals had to have their flesh held down. Is it so different for us?

What are the animals that you and I must tie down? What are some of the animals that the Church must tie down? I believe that one howling beast that we idolize in the Western Church is personal rights. This creature roars loudly in many places. He bellows and bawls if anyone dares to encroach upon his self-proclaimed dominion. As lord of his shallow domain, he curses and shouts at any intruder who would dare to challenge his faux omnipotence. His personal freedom and authority are never to be challenged. The following is an excerpt from a recent roaring of this beast heard in Anywhere Church, USA:

God, why are all these difficulties in my church? Right now, I am in the midst of some very difficult people. And I am being treated very unfairly.

Why me, God? I deserve much better than this, don't I? These people seem to have forgotten who I am. In fact, God, it seems that even You have forgotten who I am. Just what's going on?

When I became a Christian, You must admit You really got some good material. This church needs to recognize what a blessing I am. I've given this church the best years of my life. And, God, I have worked very hard for You, too. In fact, I think I've given You the best years of my life. And now this?

Don't I deserve Your favor? Can't You do something about all those awful people who are causing me such pain? The cross is not what I became a follower for. After all, I have my rights. I expect the promises that are due me.

The Song of the Brazen Altar

What do I have to do to stop this pain, God? I feel like I'm being crucified for nothing. I demand my rights. I'm a child of the King. How can I get out of this? Do you want me to scream at the enemy some more? Or shall I sing praise and worship songs until I get what I want? How can I make You do what I want?

After all, aren't You supposed to be my "Shield and Butler?" Oops, I meant Buckler!

Does this sound familiar? Oh, Singer, what has happened to those silent singers who come to *give* to God—expecting nothing? Where is the Bride who will sing of her love, motivated by her passion for Him, and Him alone? I believe you will find her at the brazen altar, quietly binding her animals to the cross.

Haven't we become deceived by the howling of such beasts? Has the Church made God a heavenly butler from whom anything can be ordered? Have we presumed to command God to fulfill every desire, every whim? Have you? That attitude is in direct opposition to the lesson of the brazen altar. The words of the song of the brazen altar are these: *I am not my own.*

This altar sings of Jesus' crucifixion. You see, Singer, Jesus demanded none of His rights from His Father:

Think of yourselves the way Christ Jesus thought of himself. He had equal status with God but didn't think so much of himself that he had to cling to the advantages of that status no matter what. Not at all. When the time came, he set aside the privileges of deity and took on the status of a slave, became human! Having become human, he stayed human. It was an incredibly humbling process. He didn't claim special privileges. Instead, he lived a selfless, obedient life and then died a selfless, obedient death—and the worst kind of death at that: a crucifixion.

Philippians 2:5-8, MES

That same attitude of worship must be sung through us. So, at the brazen altar, our incessant dictating and demanding must be crucified.

But these deep-seated attitudes do not easily crawl onto the altar. And so, this altar must have horns upon which to bind our animals. As an act of worship, we will have to bind our rights to this altar of sacrifice. Howling, these beasts must be executed.

How are these animals killed? I think you are beginning to know. God uses difficult circumstances, unjust accusations, tribulations and unfairness, just to mention a few. That should sound familiar.

You cannot sing silently without this brazen altar of the cross. So learn to ignore the screams. Let every animal of personal rights have its hour upon the altar. Let them all go.

Leonard Ravenhill expressed it this way:

The Christian who knows he has been crucified with Christ...

> *- has no ambition and so has nothing to be jealous about*
> *- has no reputation and so has nothing to fight about*
> *- has no possessions and so has nothing to worry about*
> *- has no rights and therefore cannot suffer wrong*

He is already dead and so no one can kill him.

Leviticus 21:21 calls this sacrifice *"the bread of...God."* It seems God is fed by such willing passion. His Kingdom within you is greatly expanded by such a glorious display of love. Your smallest victory over these animals is His feast.

Why? Because He sees Jesus in it.

With such a sacrifice, all whining and murmuring will be muted. Fretting will cease. All those beastly animals will become the quiet ashes of worship.

Then there will be silence. Having wrestled before God, we will learn this most important melody—that of surrender, of losing. You see, losing, or surrender, is essential for all would-be silent singers. Like the immensity of the Old Testament brazen altar, all other acts of worship can be contained within learning to lose.

For the most part, this *learning to lose* is uncultivated treasure. We prefer the gain of stimulation and the relentless din of tickled ears. The enormous strength gained in losing is, for the most part, ignored. Yet, Singer, you will find that in the silence of your losses, God is composing a main theme of your symphony of worship.

Can you hear Jesus singing these words right now?

If any man will come after me, let him ... take up his cross and follow me.   Matthew 16:24 , KJV

Consummately orchestrated by God, the brazen altar's theme of losing is to become preeminent in *all* worship. Not everyone will go to this altar. Seekers of silent music will. Will you be one of them?

You may be sure, O Singer, that if you do aspire to learn Calvary's song here at the brazen altar, you will possess, amid all the troubles of the world, a joyful resignation and rest. Indeed, yours will be an ever-deepening inner communion with the singing Christ. In exquisite silence and surrender, the profound joining will be accomplished.

Will any sound break the stillness? Will any proclamation mark the sacrifice, the surrender? Yes. The notes of a trumpet will break the hush. In the Old Testament, the tenth chapter of Numbers described it:

> *You shall blow the trumpets over your burnt offerings and over your sacrifices of well-being; they shall serve as a reminder on your behalf before the LORD your God. I am the LORD your God.*
> Numbers 10:10, NRS

God decreed that the sacrifice of every animal tied upon the brazen altar would be marked by the sound of a trumpet's blast. Every animal's bloody death upon this altar was announced by the poignant sounding of a trumpet.

Upon being consumed by the flames, the remains of the charred carcass were carefully watched by the priests. At the precise moment that the last few ashes of the offering fell through the grate of the brazen altar, a trumpet's cry would announce to the world the blessed message: It is finished!

Singer, at every death of every animal within you that demands its own rights, a note of Christ's triumph is played through you. The sound of that singular trumpet proclaims the song of His cross: *It's finished! It IS finished*!

Only at the brazen altar can this victorious note of Golgotha be played deep within you. Will you learn the silent song of losing, of surrender? Then, bend low, Singer, and embrace your cross.

A Prayer at the Brazen Altar

Lord, I am one who has a demanding voice.
It is the voice of an animal.
I always insist on my own rights, my own privileges.
I am easily incited to warring when I am denied anything.
Help me to learn to lose.

Help me to embrace the silent song *of this altar.*
Help me not to demand special privileges.
Help me to lay down my beastly avarice and daily lift my cross, that I might,
in the silence with Jesus, sing, like a trumpet, the triumphant note of His victorious song:

It is finished!

And then, draw me nearer.

Chapter Seven

The Song of the Mirrored Laver

"And you shall set the laver between the tabernacle of meeting and the altar."
(Exodus 40:7)

$\mathcal{S}$himmering in the brilliant flames of the brazen altar stood the *brazen laver,* and its flashing beauty was indescribable. Throughout both the day and the night, the reflection of the brazen altar's ceaseless fire sparkled in the highly polished surfaces of this laver. The clear water contained within this instrument of worship celebrated one theme: cleanness. Having a large upper basin and a saucer-like foot, the laver is the place for you, silent Singer, to be washed from head to toe.

Though specific measurements and details were given for most of the furnishings of the Old Testament Tabernacle, the laver's exact size was not communicated by God. The implication is quite clear: The truths contained within this holy basin are limitless. They are immeasurable. To the seeker of silent music, the brazen laver's song is fathomless. It has no end.

What does the laver sing of? It sings of God's revealed Word and its incredible cleansing power.

In the midst of this arid desert, God's laver provides clear water for His beloved worshiper. Like a flash flood, His Word becomes a stream in the wilderness. His Word is a rhapsody of rain for the thirsty singer. His Word, poured out upon you,

here in the outer court of your spirit, is meant to refresh and bathe you:

> *You are already clean because of the word which I*
> *have spoken to you.*   John 15:3

> *... that He might sanctify and cleanse her with the*
> *washing of water by the word.*   Ephesians 5:26

The Church, Jesus' silent music in the earth, is to
be bathed in the laver. You can learn no more of
worship's silent songs until you have been washed
by His words. Don't you know that the Scriptures
are the libretto of God? Singer, how can you sing if
you do not know the words? And how can you
know the words unless you read them and practice
them every day?

In the Old Testament Tabernacle, the priests
could not enter into the tent of intimacy without
first washing at this laver. God has set this laver at
the entrance to the Holy Place as a guardian of the
treasures of silent worship that await within.

Singer, do you come to be washed? Will you
choose to sit with a lap full of His Scriptures?

Because of the many trials that God allows to
nurture your silent music, your feet and hands may
become soiled. This soil is from the pollution of
your attitudes, attitudes that are revealed in your
harsh responses to others. You know, Singer, the

unkind and unthinking remarks you make. His Word alone is the detergent for such dirt.

You will need to be cleansed again and again from your grimy habits, unclean behaviors and muddy attitudes. Your soiled hands and feet will need to continually yield to the fresh moisture of His touch.

What held the cleansing water? For the Tabernacle of Moses, the Israelite women who had been emancipated from Pharaoh donated their brass mirrors to create the brazen laver. These looking glasses had been brought out of Egypt as part of the spoils of their redemption.

> *And he made the laver of brass, and the foot of it of brass, of the looking-glasses of the women assembling.* Exodus 38:8, KJV

The laver was made from surrendered mirrors, and, Singer, your own redemption experience has provided you with the raw materials to donate for the construction of such a laver of worship in your life. As the Lord continues to compose His singing presence within you, you will have to surrender something precious that you have brought as treasure out of Egypt — *your* mirror.

Why does God want mirrors? The sole purpose of a mirror is to facilitate the act of looking at oneself. We like to look at ourselves. If you disagree, try to go even one day without looking in a mirror. You and I are fascinated with our own likeness. We are quite enamored with our own image and all of its possibilities. We daily contemplate our own appearance, assessing our abilities and bemoaning our weaknesses.

As we gaze into our own hungry reflection, our reaction can be one of two extremes. We can either love or loathe the image. We can admire or deplore what we see. Whether we look with self-pity or with arrogance, the focus of our beholding is *self*. Either way, we are focused on ourselves!

A wise man once said that self is so subtle, so cunning, that it would do anything for attention. Singer, your self would rather be anything but *ignored*. Both ends of the spectrum of self (pride and pity) are simply an old mirror that we've brought out of Egypt.

Do I mean that we are really supposed to learn to ignore ourselves? Yes, that is the song of the laver. Why? Because this insatiable preoccupation with our own desires and fears perpetuates only one thing—selfishness.

It cannot be so for those who desire to sing *silent songs* of worship. God loves you far too much for that. His merciful desire is to set you free from your mirrored prison. He wants you to refocus. He wants you to look at another image—the image of Jesus. God is undaunted in His passion for you, so He wants you to surrender your paltry old Egyptian looking glass for a new mirror, the mirror of His Word.

Into your hands He places the image of Another upon whom you are to gaze. Gaze at Him, Singer! You will discover what God looks like by looking in the mirror of His Word. His Word, Jesus, is a portrait of His love. His Word is a reflection of your Beloved. Look at *Him* and be changed.

We all, with open face beholding as in a glass the glory of the Lord, are changed into the same image.
2 Corinthians 3:18 , KJV

Oh, Singer, look in your hand. That small image you see reflected in your own corroded looking glass isn't who you were purchased to be. That is only a mask that you have hidden behind. By gazing into the water of God's Word, you can have your old mask washed away.

Yes, your weaknesses will groan at their hideous appearance when they're revealed, but in the holy cleansing, your secret self-love can be uncovered and changed. So, come to the laver and allow yourself to be stripped like a child and washed clean in God's water. In the bathing, quietly agree to see yourself as you really are. God already knows.

Here at the laver, let Him tenderly scrub you.

A Prayer at the Mirrored Laver

Lord, help me.
Like a child at the end of a day of summer play, I
don't want to stop what I'm doing to get in the
tub.
Why should I?
After all, I just had a bath yesterday!

But, Jesus, in the twilight, call me to Your porch
where the cool water awaits me.

And as I slide down into the pool of Your Word,
soak away the childish dirt of the day.

I want to be clean for Your tent.

Then, draw me nearer.

Chapter Eight

The Song of the Golden Pillars

"And you shall make for the screen five pillars of acacia wood, and overlay them with gold."
(Exodus 26:37)

aving passed though the Outer Court, we find ourselves drawn to the entrance of the holy tent: the *golden pillars* of the tent of worship.

The entrance to the tent was called *the hanging*, the linen wall we saw in Chapter 4. This curtain, or hanging, was embroidered with the same quartet of gospel colors used at the gate and throughout the Tabernacle—blue, purple, scarlet and white. It was located on the east side of the tent, just as the gate to the Outer Court was. And just as the gate was the only entrance to the Outer Court, this was the only way into the tent.

Standing just outside the tent, you may experience a certain hesitation as you prepare to enter. This is a God-given awe. For this entrance is guarded by pillars covered in pure gold.

The Outer Court of your silent music has been fashioned of brass, witnessed by the brazen altar and the brazen laver. But now gold will be included in the building of God's habitation:

In this you greatly rejoice, though now for a little while you may have had to suffer grief in all kinds of trials. These have come so that your faith—of greater worth than gold, which perishes even though refined by fire—may be proved genuine and may result in praise, glory and honor when Jesus Christ is revealed.

1 Peter 1:6-7, NRS

Here, as you prepare to enter the Lord's tent, He will instruct you in the *silent song* of faith, faith that is as pure as gold.

Gold has many splendid qualities. It is luminous and brilliant. It is highly prized and was one of the first metals ever to attract man's attention. Anthropologists tell us that men have always thought themselves blessed of God simply by their possession of anything gold.

Widely dispersed throughout the earth's crust, this most precious metal is noncorrodible and virtually indestructible. Gold is extremely valuable. The entire global economy was originally based on what was known as "the gold standard." As you and I know, men never seem to have enough of this glorious metal.

Singer, God has *already* placed within you a spiritual deposit of the purest form of this element. Buried in your spirit is a vein of golden faith. It is Jesus' very own faith. Into your feeble earthy dust, God the Father has literally sown the imperishable faith of His own Son. We should tremble at the majesty of that profound act.

The Song of the Golden Pillars

Singer, when you gave your life to the Lord, He carefully pressed a golden spike of pure faith into your awaiting heart. You don't have to wonder if you have enough faith for something. It is already there, this golden vein of worship.

But, what God has placed within you must be mined. The gold must be extracted. And the process will be costly. As you draw nearer to the Source of *silent music*, your song of faith will be tried, tested and purified over and over again.

How is the priceless treasure of golden faith extracted? In its raw form, gold is encased in craggy boulders. Because of the bulk of the rock and earth surrounding it, the gold must be broken and dramatically reduced in size if it is to be recovered. The particles, or flakes, or nuggets, are crushed until they are approximately one five-hundredth of an inch in diameter or finer. In other words, they become almost like dust.

There will be times, Singer, when the events of your life will seem to bring one crushing blow after another. It may seem that there is nothing in your life but testings. You may even begin to doubt that you have any faith at all. But when your tears saturate the dust into which your face has been driven, stop weeping for a moment and *listen*. There, in the midst of the pain, purified, golden notes of silent music are being extracted from the deposit of the authentic faith deep in your heart.

The silent composition continues. The Maestro is *still* at work. A golden aria of genuine faith is being written. Forged in the agony of the testing, divine music (your faith) *is* being strengthened.

Once the particles of golden dust have been crushed, they are ready for the refining process. The refiner's fire must purify every particle of the mined vein:

> *He will purify the sons of Levi,*
> *And purge them as gold and silver,*
> *That they may offer to the* LORD
> *An offering of righteousness.*   Malachi 3:3

In its natural form, gold that has been through the initial refining process yields a product called *bullion*. Though it has been through both crushing and fire, gold bullion is still impure and must be processed further. Next, the bullion must be melted in a furnace and then immediately poured into earthen vessels.

Think of that! Gold is placed into a clay pot. Jesus' crushing yielded golden faith that was poured into a clay pot, and the clay pot He wants to fill is *you.*

The process continues. Once inside the earthen vessel, a strong and powerful blast of air is bubbled through the clay pot. Could this be like the sound of the rushing, mighty wind that came at Pentecost? Do you see, Singer? As you submit to the mining and refining of the divine vein within you, the Holy Spirit of God is breathed through your life.

With the *processing* comes the *power* of God's own faith. Only those who have known the process possess the spiritual ears to hear this uncanny melody. Genuine faith can sing through the fire and the wind.

The genuine faith that is buried deep within you has much fear and distrust to overcome in you. It will take a lifetime to extract and refine His faith residing in you. But, Singer, take heart. God is patient, and He knows that you are only dust. You may be dust, but you are *His* dust, carrying *His* faith.

Listen. Hear His wonderful song of faith within you:

> *"In this godless world you will continue to experience difficulties. But take heart! I've conquered the world."* John 16:33, MES

Jesus knows this way, the way that you now take, and when He has tried you, *His* faith will come forth in you as pure gold.

A Prayer at the Entrance of the Golden Pillars

Lord, my nursery songs of worship have been orchestrated in brass.

My primary lessons have been practiced.

But now Your mature, golden tones are yet to be extracted from me.

Help me to submit to the lifelong refining process, to momentary trials that may seem long, so that my silent song *of faith may become genuine, twenty-four carat worship for Your glory.*

Then, draw me nearer still.

Chapter Nine

The Song of the Tent Roof

*"Morever you shall make the tabernacle with
ten curtains of fine woven linen; and blue,
purple, and scarlet thread; with artistic designs
of cherubim you shall weave them.
"You shall also make curtains of goats' hair, to
be a tent over the tabernacle. ...
"You shall also make a covering of ram's skins
dyed red for the tent, and a covering of
badger skins above that."*
(Exodus 26:1, 7 and 14)

*A*s the Great Composer continues to write His anthems within your heart, He bids you to draw nearer. He is wooing you, urging you to come closer, to come deeper. The golden pillars are behind you. Now, He desires to bring you into His *tent*. It is the place beneath His wings, where His silent music will be ever sweeter.

In the Tabernacle that Moses built, God commanded four heavy mantles to be placed as coverings to His habitation. This dome of curtains and coverings blanketed His tent. Your Tabernacle of silent songs will be draped in these skirts, too:

Do you not know that you are the temple of God and that the Spirit of God dwells in you?
1 Corinthians 3:16

In biblical culture, the spreading of a cover over someone was symbolic of giving protection. If the act occurred between a man and a woman, it was a proposal of marriage. It declared the giving of oneself forever. Ruth knew this when she lay at the feet of Boaz and tenderly requested, *"I am Ruth thine handmaid: spread therefore thy skirt over thine handmaid"* (Ruth 3:9). Her acceptance of the covering of Boaz signified that a covenant had been entered into. Now, God desires to blanket your silent music in a quartet of quilts and covers.

The Tabernacle's coverings had four layers. Four distinct blankets were stretched over *all* of the intimacies of interior worship. And the layers of God's first Tabernacle ceilings are to become our garments as well. Singer, will you receive the covenant of these mantles?

Badger Skins

The outermost covering of Moses' Tabernacle was made of badger skins, skins that were clearly visible from a great distance. But were these taken from the animal we know as a badger today? This word *badger* can also be translated *sea animal*, *dolphin* or *porpoise*. It is a general Hebrew term for marine creatures. Archeologists tell us that species such as those indicated in the context of the Scriptures were plentiful in the Red Sea near Sinai in Moses' day.

These marine animal skins were, according to the Septuagint, a drab blue-gray color. They were not particularly impressive to look at, and neither were they considered particularly valuable or beautiful. In a similar way, the prophet Isaiah declares that Jesus took on the drab skin of humanity:

The Song of the Tent Roof

He had no beauty or majesty to attract us to him.
Isaiah 53:2 , NIV

In other words, God the Father chose that the outermost covering of Jesus' silent music would be ordinary, not ostentatious. Humility was the skin that would be the outer blanket of God's glory.

Singer, the silent music of your own interior tabernacle must be like the outer covering of the Tabernacle. It must be clothed in humility. How? You and I must stop trying to be known. That is ambition. We must stop trying to be counted in the company of those who are honored for their abilities or ministries. Our aim must be to disarm all such ambitions by embracing any ordinariness that God permits.

Four distinct mantles will cover you, and the very first of these must be a willingness to be humble, ordinary. Learn, oh, precious Singer, to say little and do much without wondering if you've been noticed by others. Learn to receive from God, not from men. Embrace this truth. This is the outermost covering of the worship tent—allowing God to stretch a mantle of humble obscurity over your life.

The badger skins that served as the outermost curtain of the tent also served to cover the feet of the Old Testament worshiper. In the eastern Sinai Peninsula, these skins were the standard material for making sandals and priestly shoes. These shoes were soft-soled and moccasin-like.

What does this imply? It shows us that a silent singer must also be shod in humility. Your walk, not just your appearance, must be authentic. You must walk gently, with extravagant softness. Harshness, cruelty or defensiveness cannot be upon your feet. You may not tread upon others to achieve any perceived destiny. You may not stomp your way into any promise. That is not the walk of a silent singer.

Yes, every place that the soles of your feet tread *is* God's promise to you. But you must wear the same kind of shoes that Jesus wore, quiet and unassuming. As you cover the terrain between yourself and God's promises, you are to wear the gentle, silent shoes of a worshiping priest, shoes that are soft-soled.

Jesus never demanded His destiny from His Father. Rather, He walked in soft shoes. He walked in faithfulness and obedience, trusting His Father for the outcome. That is the walk of humility.

Singer, if you wear these shoes, God promises you what He promised both Israel and His Son:

Child, your shoes will not wear out, even in the rocky harshness of the wilderness—as long as you keep them on. Bruises are not only possible, but probable. But I, your God, promise that more than your shoes not failing, YOU won't wear out in the wilderness as you're learning to sing this gentle song. In fact, your willingness to walk softly and humbly before Me is absolutely irresistible to Me. For when I watch your humility and your willingness to be tender, I hear such magnificent music. As a silent singer, what you do softly and for My eyes alone may never impress the world or even the church. Nonetheless, your actions and tender walk are proof that you have allowed Me to cover your tent with the badger skins of humility. It is proof of My composing presence within you.

Ram Skins Dyed Red

Beneath the outer covering of badger skins, God placed a second ceiling of silent worship. It was a cover of ram skins dyed red. This was the central covering of the Tabernacle. These crimson skins declared a singular truth—sacrificial love. Your *silent song* will be as empty as the sound of a clanging cymbal without authentic sacrificial love.

Jesus' incredible love for you expressed itself in bloody death. It killed Him to love you. And it will kill *you* to love others sacrificially.

As in the Old Testament Tabernacle, this ballad of sacrificial love will be the central cover of your interior tabernacle. What does that mean? It means loving the unlovable. It means loving your enemies. It means you can't get angry at what people say or do. You must let them talk. You do God's will and love the people around you. You must learn to be loving to everyone without counting on or demanding their love in return.

To be a silent singer, you must be willing to sing God's love songs to *all* people—the pleasant and the unpleasant alike—no matter what they say or do. God delights in every note of this love song that continues to give and give and give, expecting nothing in return:

> *"You have heard that it was said, You shall love your neighbor and hate your enemy. But I say to you, love your enemies, and pray for those who ... persecute you, that you may be sons of your Father in Heaven."*   Matthew 5:43-45

Singer, beneath the outermost mantle of ordinariness and humility, will you wear the blanket of crucified love?

Goats' Hair

Under the badger skins of humility and the ram skins of love, a third cover stretched over the tent of worship, a curtain of goats' hair. In Old Testament times, goats were used as sin offerings. And Jesus was this sin offering for you.

Singer, rejoice! These goat skins establish that your silent music will forever be covered by Jesus' sacrifice. *His* sacrifice, *His* death, *His* worthiness ... these attributes alone have secured your access to the Tabernacle.

Why do I remind you of this basic truth now? Because the accuser of silent songsters loves to remind seekers of their own depravity, particularly here in the tent. When the accuser would whisper that you aren't good enough to enter God's presence or when a sense of your own destitution overwhelms you, look up. Lift a trembling hand to point out the goats' hair curtain that will forever cover your relationship with God.

Covering your pitiable inadequacy is Christ's offering on your behalf. He has paid for your worship. Because of Jesus, you *are* the righteousness of God. So sing with *certainty* beneath the music of the goats' hair curtain:

> *For he hath made him to be sin for us, who knew no sin; that we might be made the righteousness of God in him.*　　2 Corinthians 5:21, KJV

O beloved Singer, your song has been purchased and the visual record of that transaction is preserved in God's dwelling place forever. You belong in the tent.

Covered by the three other mantles, a final curtain with cherubim embroidered upon it was the innermost ceiling of the tent of worship. Intricately woven with blue, purple and scarlet upon a white linen background, cherubim stretched out their heavenly wings to tenderly cover the Holy Place. Again, it was made of linen, the same fabric as the curtain of the Outer Court, the same fabric that blankets every intimate act of worship.

When once you set your feet within the Holy Place, you will be drawn to look upward. Go on, look up. There is spectacular beauty just above your head.

Behold! As you gaze heavenward within this holy tent, colorfully embroidered into the linen layer of the roof are winged cherubim. Their colors portray Jesus: blue — His grace; purple — His triumph; and scarlet — His service.

The multicolored wings of this innermost ceiling declare a more wonderful truth. They sing of Christ's protecting lordship over you.

Singer, beneath the feathery wings, Jesus is singing. He is singing His song of protection *into* you. Listen:

You who sing in the silence and shadow of My presence,

I am your refuge;
trust Me and you'll be safe.
I will deliver you
from the cunning of the fowler.
My outstretched feathers will gently
touch and guard your music.
Don't be afraid of anything,
night or day;
prowling pestilence in the dark
or the scorch of the noonday sun.
Others may stop singing all around you,
but your soliloquy will keep soaring.
You will stand quietly confident, merely watch-
ing and humming from a distance.
I will protect you because you have let Me be
your tent.   Psalm 91: 1-10, my paraphrase

Singer, sing! You are safe.

A quartet of blankets covers God's habitation of silent music. What are they? They are a worshiper's willingness to sing, even in the gray-drab music of obscurity, sacrificial love that loves even the unlovable, amazing confidence to sing because of the Scapegoat's eternal covering, and a knowledge of Jesus' outstretched feathery pinions of protection. These are the robes of the tent of *silent music.*

A Prayer Under the Tent Roof

Lord, You've brought me into Your sacred tent.

Help me now to look up, see and wear these blankets of worship as my own soft garments.

These four mantles are part of the inheritance You've willed to me.

You've prepared me, and now You clothe me.

In the stillness of this robing, I bless You.

Oh, draw me nearer.

Chapter Ten

The Harmony of the Tabernacle Walls

"And for the tabernacle you shall make the boards of acacia wood, standing upright."
(Exodus 26:15)

he soft ceilings of the dome of the Tabernacle were supported by *walls of wood*. The scaffold that upheld the four soft ceilings of the tent of Moses' Tabernacle was an infrastructure of forty-eight acacia wood beams, or boards. These stood perpendicular to the desert floor. Then the four soft covers were layered over this wooden framework.

Each board of the framework was to be fashioned identically. All of them would need time on the woodworker's bench. Each piece of lumber for the framework of the tent was to be straight and strong. All of them were to be planed, sanded and carefully handled by both the workmen and the master builder. Once each piece of wood had been completely prepared, it was then covered in pure gold. The golden boards then became one as they stood hand-in-hand to support the glory of the tent.

In this way, God was building His habitation, and God *is* building His habitation — in us.

Do you hear the growing music within, Singer? There is a grand crescendo in the symphony. Until now, God has orchestrated your circumstances and your music to make you a soloist of *silent songs*. Patiently, He has singled you out to create linen from raw flax. He has brought you from outside the gate and into His courts. He has begun to paint the blue, purple, scarlet and white melodies of Jesus into your character. At His brazen altar you have learned Calvary's song. Jesus' song of faith is growing continually purer through your refining. Washing in the laver of His Word has begun to cleanse away your selfish dissonance. And upon your shoulders rest the four-layered melodies of His tent.

Do you feel that you are unique? You should, for you are.

But the wider truth is this: God is *also* perfecting this exact symphony in a multitude of others. In fact, He is working in millions of others. You are not alone in this. The school of silent music is filled with hungry seekers.

Why is this? It is because you were never meant to sing alone. You were meant for the choir! So now, it is time for you to learn to sing with others. Here, within the walls of the tabernacle, you are to learn to sing in *harmony.*

As any musician knows, soloists can be quite self-centered. Prima donnas are always plentiful. But, as in any school of music, isolation from other musicians is no way to fully learn the art of song. You have to learn the art of singing with others. Forming a pleasant, consistent whole community is God's intention. He wants a conservatory of duets, trios, quartets and quintets. You were made for such polyphony.

Jesus, our pattern, didn't isolate Himself. As the Tabernacle of God, He slept body-to-body in the same room with twelve blue-collar workers. He put up with their body odor. He washed their feet. He even knew that some of them would eventually betray Him. But He sang with them anyway.

He willingly shared His time, space and music with *all* of the people He encountered. He experienced the press of hot, sweaty crowds. People stepped on His feet. He welcomed messy little children onto His lap. And He quietly hummed through it all.

Jesus was touchable; He was accessible.

Yes, He spent solo time singing to His Father, but He always rejoiced to touch and be touched by people. He unselfishly made contact and He became a part of, not apart from, others.

How can we begin to sing in real harmony with others the way Jesus did? The golden walls of the Tabernacle have much to teach us.

First, each board in the wall contributed to the wholeness of the structure. The tent could not stand with just one plank. God's habitation required all of the boards. In this same way, God desires to sing in the whole community. Where two or three begin to sing His music, He is there! He sits down in the midst of His choir of seekers to rejoice with them. He wants them all to know the wonder of His music.

Sadly, our culture struggles with the concept of "the good of the whole." And honestly, sometimes we Christians do, too. "What's in it for me?" is not what God teaches in His interior Tabernacle. His theme is "What's best for My whole Body?"

Musicians of excellence know this "principle of the whole." They understand that many must play subordinate parts so that the entire orchestra will overflow with harmony. And they know (as often we do not seem to) that the hardest instrument for anyone to play is second fiddle.

Yet this is precisely what God wants to teach us. He wants us to learn to patiently prefer one another, rejoicing as God promotes someone else into the spotlight. He wants us to graciously allow the success of others to be accomplished before our own. He knows that when such harmony is heard, the entire orchestra is honored. When God's harmony is present, each silent singer derives his meaning from the habitation as a whole, not the other way around:

> *For just as in one body we have many members,*
> *but not all the members have the same function,*
> *so the many of us form one body in Christ, while*
> *each is related to all others as a member.*
>
> Romans 12:4, MLB

To understand how challenging harmony can be, let's investigate the type of lumber that God specifically chose for the tabernacle walls—shittim wood. Though they would eventually be covered in gold, the forty-eight boards of the Tabernacle walls were originally hewn from shittim wood, a lackluster lumber that comes from the acacia tree. In fact, this is the only type of wood that was used in any part of the Tabernacle. Trees and wood, you remember, are scriptural pictures of humanity.

God required a specific wood from a specific tree, and it seems that the acacia tree was His tree of choice. Why was that?

For one thing, acacia trees, growing to a height of approximately twenty feet, were common to the Sinai region. These trees, according to Isaiah 41:19, were associated with bringing joy to the desert. They are crooked, spindly trees with not much available lumber because of their short trunks and their many knotholes and branches. They are misshapen and twisted even as saplings. Still, this was God's choice for the lumber to be used in the Tabernacle. He did not choose the straight cedar or the strong oak, but rather the gnarly acacia.

Isn't that a picture of us, Singer? We are all full of knotholes, with gnarly, twisted branches. Yet God chooses us to be His corporate habitation for silent worship.

Isn't that amazing? Crooked, common, isolated

trees, crooked even from birth, are to be crafted into an infrastructure in which God will sing.

The Bible calls this crookedness *"iniquity."* Singer, do you know what iniquities are? They are your crooked bents toward certain sins. Iniquities are born in us through our parents. They are in us even as seedlings. We are prone to specific weaknesses that were found in our ancestors. These propensities are passed on to our children and grandchildren. They are the specific sin tendencies that are unique to you and your family tree.

Is your father hot-tempered? It isn't because he's Italian. Is your mother stingy? It isn't because her roots are in Scotland. It is because of iniquitous tendencies toward specific sins that are passed on from generation to generation.

What about you? Do you, with chagrin, recognize any negative behaviors in yourself that make you cringe to say, "I'm acting just like my mother!" What about your children? Does little Johnny's short fuse remind you of yourself? You are looking at iniquities.

Character iniquities are passed along to your seed just like physical traits. Blue eyes beget blue eyes. Broad shoulders beget broad shoulders. And iniquities beget iniquities.

As unnerving as this all may be, these bents in us can be redeemed by God for His habitation. The people in your church are loaded with iniquities, but so are you. The good news is that Jesus was *"bruised for our iniquities"* (Isaiah 53:5).

Isn't that an astounding statement? Because of Jesus, God can use each funny, gnarly, bent tree. He can transform each one. But how? How can a bent tree become a straight board to stand upright and in order in His house? The answer is found in the natural processing of lumber from the acacia tree.

First, the acacia tree had to be severed from the earth. These crooked trees had sent their roots deep into the desert sand from their very birth. Just trying to survive, they drew up any moisture they could find from the muddy waters far below the surface.

Be honest, Singer. Isn't there still much of you that drinks in the things of this world? God proposes to sever your roots to that old thirst. He is doing the same in those around you. Old sources must end for you and for them, so that He might fit you both into place in His habitation.

First the acacia tree must be felled, and your tree must be felled too. Saul of Tarsus knew such a moment. Acts declares that Saul *"fell"*:

> *And he [Saul] fell to the earth, and heard a voice saying unto him, Saul, Saul, why persecutest thou me.* Acts 9:4 , KJV

With one sharp blow of the Lord's axe, Saul fell, and the new tree that came up in its place was Paul. Then God spent many years carefully and painstakingly fashioning Paul into a productive board for the early Church.

All silent singers destined for God's habitation will know such a moment. We will be felled. Then, having been felled, we will lie in the desert sand, no longer able to suck the earth for our nourishment. As we lie there in the dust of the desert, we might wonder if God is trying to destroy us. But He's not! We are to have a new destiny, a new thirst, a thirst that cannot ever be completely fulfilled without becoming a part of His whole habitation, the Church.

What happens next to one of these trees? Once harvested, the tree's twisted branches are removed. Since all of the acacia's branches are crooked, a great part of the tree is thus pruned away. This same thing happens with you. Once you were a fine, many-branched tree. Now, here in the wilderness, it seems that you are no more than a runty little stump!

Let me inquire: Has God ever removed anything from you? Has He ever withdrawn you from public ministry? Has He ever taken away something that you prized? Has He ever reduced your sphere of influence or allowed your reputation to be attacked? If so, rise up and call Him blessed, for He is pruning you to allow for new growth, and this will result in good for His Church.

Yes, it *is* humiliating—quite so. But didn't you say that you wanted all of God's *silent songs*? Well then, listen to the music He sings as He wields His pruning shears:

> *I am the true vine, and my Father is the gardener. He cuts off every branch in me that bears no fruit, while every branch that does bear fruit he prunes so that it will be even more fruitful.*
>
> John 15:1, NIV

God is pruning us so that we can bring forth fruit.

After all of that, surely the acacia wood was finally ready for its destiny? No, Singer, there is more. There was the problem of sap.

You are full of sap, acacia tree. You are still full of the moisture that you drank from your old life. So you will have to lie in the hot desert sun until all of the sap of the earth that is still within you has dried up. Your old-life sap must evaporate. The things of your earthly nature have to dry up. Who you once were has to dry up, and this takes time:

> *Put to death, therefore, whatever belongs to your earthly nature: sexual immorality, impurity, lust, evil desires and greed, which is idolatry. Be-*

109

cause of these, the wrath of God is coming. You used to walk in these ways, in the life you once lived. But now you must rid yourselves of all such things as these: anger, rage, malice, slander, and filthy language from your lips.

Colossians 3:5-8, NIV

Being weaned away from the old, earthy nature takes time. So, little stump, you must lie there until you are no longer green wood. Just as you had to remain submerged in the process to become flax for linen, once again this silent music requires waiting ... and seasoning.

You see, green wood that is sticky with sap will easily buckle. It will warp if it is used prematurely. One of the most dangerous things you could do in the time of seasoning would be to insist on being used prematurely. For the sake of the whole Church, usable men and women must wait until God's hand lifts them. Until then, you must lie there and dry.

How long will this take? I don't know. As long as it takes, I guess. So, Singer, learn to embrace the seasoning.

Once the tree has dried enough, the builder will search for the exact stump that He needs for His specific purpose. Yet this lopped-off trunk still requires more of His attention.

Do you mean to say that this truncated stripling

still demands the Logger's skills? Yes, there are numerous knotholes buried within the wood that must be addressed.

What exactly are knotholes? They are places in the wood that have become hardened, almost petrified sometimes. Knotholes are created when the base of a branch has become embedded into the body of the wood. The trunk of the tree has grown around the branch, producing an encased knot.

These are the spots of great weakness in the tree. Insects will make a home in a knothole, and if they are not removed, any lumber made from that portion of the tree may break in a time of stress.

Singer, what are the knotholes in your heart? What piercing wounds have caused you to wall up and retreat?

Knotholes are usually begun when a tree is tender and young. As a sapling, how were you hurt? When you were young, were you rejected by your father, your mother? Were you abused or neglected? Is there, beneath all your façade, a wounded child, an abused child, a petrified soul?

Early wounds are the beginnings of knotholes, and those solidified knots can cause calluses around your heart. The archenemy of your music can easily penetrate your wounds. Insects of unforgiveness can burrow deep into the pulp of your being. The end result is that you will eventually become petrified, hardened. Then, afraid to trust and fearful of another wound, you will find yourself retreating from fellowship.

But, Singer, you were born for fellowship and harmony. So Jesus comes to you to soften your heart and tenderly remove the knotholes. Let Him do it, for your future as His habitation is at stake.

God has no favorites. He will handle and fashion each board for the walls of the Tabernacle. He will do it in His time and in His own way. Although each board has many knotholes, God will patiently and mercifully deal with each one.

Dealing with knotholes requires mercy, the mercy of a tree-surgeon. During the necessary surgery, have mercy on yourself, as God has. During the surgeries others are undergoing, have mercy on them too, as God has. Learning to show mercy is the sweet sound of harmony, and singing in harmony brings unity.

Yes, there is a place in the golden wall for you that only you can fill. No one else can fulfill your unique destiny—only you. But God has an equally important place for many others as well. Receive and show God's mercy, acacia stump.

Paul instructs us on how to be patient and merciful toward all the other acacia trees that are in the same church:

Summing it all up, friends, I'd say you'll do best by filling your minds and meditating on things

> *true, noble, reputable, authentic, compelling, gracious—the best, not the worst; the beautiful, not the ugly; things to praise, not things to curse. ... Do that, and God, who makes everything work together, will work you into his most excellent harmonies.* Philippians 4:8-9, MES

All of these processes—the severing, the pruning, the seasoning—are meant to birth the gift of harmony within the Church. The Builder has purposed for you to be *a part of*, not *apart from,* His community of silent songsters. He is quite at home there:

> *Now he's using you, fitting you in brick by brick, stone by stone, with Christ Jesus as the cornerstone that holds all the parts together. We see it taking shape day after day—a holy temple built by God, all of us built into it, a temple in which God is quite at home.*
> Ephesians 2:20-22, MES

I have often wondered why God the Father did not birth His Son into an earthly family whose trade was fishing. After all, Jesus trained His followers to be fishers of men. Or, why did He not send His Son to be raised by a farming family? During His earthly ministry, Jesus taught much about the harvest. But God in His wondrous wisdom placed Jesus as apprentice to a carpenter so that He would learn to work with wood.

Think about that: wood. That's you and me. We're wood that needs considerable work, wood that is twisted and bent, wood that requires the skilled hands of the Carpenter. The wooden walls of the Tabernacle are His home, and He inhabits them individually and corporately.

When Jesus chose us as crooked trees, we were knotty and full of the sap of self. With severe mercy, He laid an axe to our roots and lovingly set forth to shape and plane our lives that we might conform to His own express image. He continues to shape His habitation today. Our responsibility is to reverberate with the *silent song* in harmony.

A Prayer at the Walls of Wood

Help me, Lord.
I am wood, full of gnarls and crookedness.
I have wounds and knotholes where I nurse the
insects of unforgiveness, bitterness and self-pity.

These flaws cause me to want to isolate myself
from Your Church.
But, behold, You have chosen me, along with
many other acacia trees,
to house Your Presence.
And my heart's cry is to honor You.

Take me, then, onto Your workbench.
Plane, sand and smooth me as You will.

Master Carpenter, make me able to sing the song
of unity and harmony that is etched into all
worshiping boards that You have designed for the
silent symphony.

And in harmony, draw us all nearer.

Chapter Eleven

The Music Inside the Tent

"The king's daughter is all glorious within."
(Psalm 45:13, KJV)

inger, you are being built into Jesus' holy habitation. Now, you and the other seeking singers in the wilderness have access to the furniture of the Holy Place. In fact, you *house* the Holy Place; no, more precisely you *are* the Holy Place — individually, yes, but corporately too. You and that plank of acacia wood that worships next to you are a chosen part of the dwelling of God.

What is *inside* this fellowship tent? It's treasure. If you were to stand, as did the priests of Moses' day, within the walls of this holy home, this conservatory of *silent song*, what would you see? The humble exterior of this tabernacle-conservatory belies her extravagant interior. On the outside, she is layered with drab animal skins, but inside she is robed in resurrection splendor. Outside she is dark and comely, but inside her beauty is unspeakable.

Light reflected in her golden acacia boards is flashing everywhere. The source of that radiating light is to your left. It is a golden lampstand. It is the only light illuminating the Holy Place. Each of the golden acacia boards radiates and reflects the splendor of this exquisite light.

Allow your eyes to explore even more of the interior of the tent. To your right, do you see the delicate golden table for food? The feast upon it is intimate, divine fellowship. The menu is Christ. Here, within this Holy Place, He will tenderly nourish all who are His.

Breathe deeply. This small, exquisite room is filled with a lovely smoke. The perfume of it is nothing like the stench of burning animals outside. No, this is the aroma of poured-out love. Its source is a narrow golden altar that stands straight ahead of you—the golden altar of incense.

Inhale, Worshiper. The perfume ascending from the golden altar of incense is intoxicating. It delights the nostrils of God. It has the scent of loving intercession. One quiet, purposeful breath of this incense both brings and gives life.

Now, look down, Singer. Amazingly, there is no floor to this structure. Although each board stands upon a solid silver socket that lifts the entire structure out of the desert sand, those who minister as *silent singers* in this tent will serve with their feet in the dust.

Then, look up. Remember the four layers of soft ceilings? Their thickness muffles any earthly noise. The silence of this narrow room is incredible. Surrounded by such wordless glory, descriptions do not come easily.

The Music Inside the Tent

This holy room is unlike any other place that you have ever seen. Most singers never want to move from this spot. But there are more *silent songs* to be learned from the worship furniture of the interior. Profound music awaits you.

Welcome into the tent of God, seeking Singer.

A Prayer on the Inside of the Tent

Lord, the songs of Your habitation within me are beginning to overtake my life more and more. Yet, as I stand here for the first time within Your tent, the silent music is gentler, no, stronger.

Teach me more, Lord!

Write the melodies of the table, of the light and of the incense into my heart.

Lord, here I am.

Draw me even nearer.

Chapter Twelve

The Song of the Fellowship Table

"You shall also make a table of acacia wood."
(Exodus 25:23)

*A*s you enter this utterly exquisite Holy Place, the *table of showbread, the fellowship table,* stands immediately to your right. Unleavened bread, chalices and dishes are presented upon this somewhat small, narrow table.

In all of Scripture, this is the first use of the word *table.* The heart of the Hebrew word for *table* means "to be extended, to spread out." What does this mean to a silent singer?

In your home, when you come to the dinner table with your family, what are your needs? You eat to satisfy your physical hunger. But don't you also hunger for something other than food? Isn't there a cry in you for something more than just the natural food? Don't you desire to connect, to communicate, to experience fellowship? Isn't the table a place where you come to listen and to be heard? Because of this, does anyone really like to eat alone?

You see, Singer, you were built with a hunger for fellowship, and not just surface fellowship, but divine conversation. You were made "to extend and spread out." You were made for the table, and the table was made for you.

Fellowship at this table is where the silent music of communion between Jesus and His Father can be heard. They are both there at table feasting and fellowshipping.

Jesus savored this fellowship. He understood the table. He ate and drank there with His Father before eternity began. He knew the immeasurable pleasure and privilege of internal fellowship with His Father. Jesus knew His Father as Abba, loving and intimate. It was such a tender, satisfying fellowship that He continued this inner dialogue with Abba all the time He was robed in flesh here on the earth. He knew it as worship, as silent music within Him.

Do you remember His words, *"I am always hearing Abba"* (John 12:50, my paraphrase)? How could this be? It was because the Father dwelt (or tabernacled) within Jesus. This interior conversation underlay all of His outward activity. He cherished this internal dialogue.

Reflect on the music of those conversations, those *silent songs* sung between Father and Son at this table of intimate fellowship. Listen in the silence. Can you hear the magnificent music that Jesus is singing: *"My Abba and I are One"* (John 10:30, my paraphrase)? It is a divine duet.

Listen very carefully to this duet. It is not the sound of authority, or power or miracles. It is not even the sound of gifts. Incredibly, it is not even the sound of worship as you and I know it. No, the sounds between Father and Son are the sounds of gentle listening, *really* listening to each other, and the fellowship of knowing, *really* knowing one another.

What does Jesus say about *you* in these conversations? Keep listening:

> *"I am in my Abba; My Abba is in me."*
> *"And you are in me, and I am in you."*
> *"Fill up your joy. Come fellowship with us."*
> John 14:10, 15:5 and Revelation 3:20-21
> (my paraphrase)

Aren't those wonderful words? You are welcome at Abba's table.

One of the holiest things a seeking singer will ever know is found at this table of fellowship, and the table is always prepared. Jesus declares that unless we eat the bread of life and drink the wine, we will have no part in Him (see John 6:53). So partake.

You see, Singer, in the deepest, most interior places of your spirit, Jesus lives unfettered. He sings and eats with His Father. Their table is prepared, and you are invited. The divine duet becomes a trio as the Holy Spirit within you sings.

I hear your questions and concerns: "How can I be in communion constantly with Jesus? I'm not always aware of His music within. It seems that I am always being caught up in the demands of daily living. I don't seem to be able to pray or sing all of the time. I have so much to do. If I don't spend my time fulfilling my obligations, how will all of it get done? I want to sit at my Master's table and pray and sing without ceasing, but I am so busy, so distracted."

I will let Brother Lawrence, a Carmelite lay-brother who lived more than three hundred years ago, address your concern. The following is an excerpt from his book, *The Practice of the Presence of God*:

> *During your meals or during any daily duty, simply lift your heart up to Him, because even the least little remembrance will please Him. You don't have to pray out loud; He's nearer than you can imagine. It isn't necessary that we stay in a church in order to remain in God's presence. We can make our heart a chapel where we can go anytime to talk to God privately. These conversations can be so loving and gentle, and anyone can have them."*
>
> (Brother Lawrence, *The Practice of the Presence of God*, [New Kensington, Pa.: Whitaker House, 1982], p. 60.)

"Martha, Martha," I can hear Jesus say, "at this table, you can learn to rest and listen" (see Luke

10:41). Jesus *did* much Himself, but all the while, He centered His interior eyes upon His Father. He listened for His Father's music amid the din of daily noise. The Father and the Son were always looking upon each other with love. They beheld each other with their eyes *and* with their ears. They are, in fact, still beholding each other—within you.

This song of the fellowship table transcends words. This communication goes far beyond mortal discourse. Prayer between the Father and the Son goes far beyond mere directives or petitions. Instead, it is composed of listening and beholding each other's *silent song*—listening, beholding and speaking *without* the clumsiness of words.

The table is a place of extension, a place to hear and be heard, a place to listen and a place to sing, a place to be present before God, a place to behold silent music:

> *If we don't know how or what to pray, it doesn't matter. He does our praying in and for us, making prayer out of our wordless sighs, our aching groans. He know us far better than we know ourselves, knows our pregnant condition, and keeps us present before God.*   Romans 8:26, MES

Beloved Singer, the song to be learned at the table is this: Silent worship is simply lovingly

129

beholding the Son within you, as He is lovingly beholding the Father. This is a simple and profound truth, to be sure, but it is also a promise of God:

> *"Therefore I am now going to allure her;*
> *I will lead her into the desert and speak tenderly*
> *to her."*   Hosea 2:14, NIV

A Prayer at the Table

Lord, the duet that I hear at this table compels me to come to the place prepared for me.

Here, in the noiseless sand, You invite me to be open.
You allow me to extend myself before You.
You invite me to listen.
You invite me to behold.

At this table, You desire that I would hear the gentle fellowship between You and our Abba. This communion of which I partake is beyond mere delight to my tongue; for my song has become what I eat and drink with You.

For such profound sustenance, I bless You with all that I am.

O Lord, draw me nearer.

Chapter Thirteen

The Song of the Unleavened Bread

*"And you shall set the showbread
on the table before Me always."*
(Exodus 25:30)

*W*hat food is being served upon the table of fellowship? The menu there is *unleavened bread*. And just what is unleavened bread? It is bread that hasn't had the opportunity to get "puffed up" yet.

To understand the significance of unleavened bread, we must first define *leaven*. Leaven in the Scriptures speaks of prideful sin. Jesus warned:

> *"Beware of the leaven of the Pharisees."*
> Matthew 16:6

What did Jesus mean by this? The Pharisees were brilliant students of the Law. Highly educated, they were self-assured in their interpretations of God's laws. They definitely knew good from evil. They fed upon such knowledge. Their dogmatic preoccupation with knowledge of good versus evil caused them to be full of themselves, puffed up:

> *Knowledge puffs up, but love builds up. The man who thinks he knows something does not yet know as he ought to know. But the man who loves God is known by God.*   1 Corinthians 8:1-3, NIV

Singer, knowledge for knowledge's sake always puffs up. It is a fruit from the forbidden tree in the garden:

> *And the LORD God commanded the man saying, Of every tree of the garden thou mayest freely eat: but of the tree of the knowledge of good and evil, thou shalt not eat of it: for in the day that thou eatest thereof thou shalt surely die.*
>
> Genesis 2:16-17, KJV

Hunger to know the *tree of good and evil* rather than to know the *Tree of Life* is the cradle of pride. To be able to have knowledge enough to judge good from evil is a heady thing. It is the song of judgment. It is the bluster of pride. Those who sing such songs rarely learn to sing *silent songs*.

Their hunger for a superiority of knowledge caused the Pharisees to continue to eat from the wrong tree. Why? Because they loved their knowledge of good and evil. They were even bold enough to dare judge the Son of God! That's how well they knew the Scriptures!

But their love of *knowledge* blinded them to a *knowledge of Life*. The very Tree of Life stood among them, laden with His fruit, but when they were confronted with His life-giving arbor of love, they preferred judgment.

Oh, Singer, let it not be so with you! Knowing

good from evil is not what is being served upon the table in the Holy Place. No, God serves the unleavened bread-fruit of love from the Tree of Life. Upon His table, only love is served, only Life is served. This unleavened bread of Jesus is what you are to present before the face of God.

How can that be done? Refuse to continue to eat from the death-tree of comparison. Comparison demands that there be a winner. Comparison lifts someone up and puts someone else down. Therefore, comparison separates.

Stop comparing your good with another's evil. White is not better than black. Men are not better than women. Black is not better than white. Women are not better than men. Stop trying to win.

Although the Pharisees were men of wisdom, they were not wise men. They could not see purity. Because their hearts were impure, they could only see impurity.

Follow the example of the Magi at Jesus' birth. When you find Christ in someone, revere His seed in that person, even if His seed is found in its infancy. Look for *the unleavened bread, Jesus,* in others.

As the Scriptures have said:

To the pure all things are pure.   Titus 1:15

A Prayer at the Unleavened Bread

Lord, help me.
I eat from the tree of the knowledge of good and evil.
I am quick to label myself, to compare myself with others.
Somehow I always want to win.

The leaven that fills me manifests itself in judgment—of myself and of others.
Both are very painful.

But the tree that stands in the center of Your habitation within me is laden with fruit, the bread of Life, the taste of love.

It is Your unleavened bread that I desire.
Help me to develop a taste for it.

And draw me nearer.

Chapter Fourteen

The Song of the Golden Lampstand

"You shall also make a lampstand of pure gold … . And six branches shall come out of its sides: three branches of the lampstand out of one side, and three branches of the lampstand out of the other side."
(Exodus 25:31-32)

Having nourished your spirit at the table of showbread, look over at the opposite side of the Holy Place. The singular source of light within this holy room is the golden lampstand. And it is magnificent. Hammered from a single talent of gold, and elaborate with inwrought fruit, it is absolutely breathtaking!

Look, Singer! The center shaft of the lampstand towers above its branches. It is the tallest. It is the root.

On either side of the root stem are three branches, making a total of six. Six is the number of man.

Having been created from a single talent of gold, these side branches are literally drawn from the side of the main shaft, or vine. It is important for you to see, Worshiper, that these branches come directly from the root. They are extracted from the sides of the center vine. Notice that to create the branches the side of the center shaft had to be split open, pierced. Only this kind of surgery would allow the birth of the branches.

Once, long ago, in a setting that we cannot fully comprehend, another surgery of sorts was performed upon a man named Adam. It seemed that Adam had been created alone. God said it was not good for him to be alone, so He determined that he should meet his wife.

Adam's wife, his bride, was to be a help to him, a delight to him. In fact, she would be his completion. But God did not have to begin making this bride from the dust, as He had with Adam. No, this wife was *in* Adam from the time he was created. She was there, *inside him*, just waiting to be revealed.

God put Adam into a deep sleep, and while Adam was in this state of utter dependence, God pierced his side. Reaching into the area near the first man's heart, the skillful Surgeon removed some of Adam's bone. His DNA then became his bride's DNA.

This was to be the foundation for his spouse. She came, not out of Adam's head, so that he could dominate her with his knowledge, or out of his feet, which might have signified that she was merely to serve him. This woman who was to become Adam's bride was taken from under his arm very near to his heart. This signifies that she was to be loved and protected by him. The bride of Adam was to be a reflection of himself—bone of his bone and flesh of his flesh (see Genesis 2:23).

Then, nearly two thousand years ago, the Father expressed to His Son the need to bring forth a Bride for Him. Jesus, the Second Adam, agreed and complied. On a Jerusalem hill, He willingly stretched Himself out upon a coarse execution stake. He spread wide His arms to give His Father access to His breast. And once again, God became Surgeon.

Would Jesus' Bride be drawn from His head to be dominated by His knowledge? Would she be drawn from His feet to merely serve Him? No, again, this spouse would come from deep within His breast. From His pierced side would issue the blood necessary to create her. She was more than just bone of His bone; she was blood of His blood.

And you are that Bride, Singer. He is the Root, and you and I are His branches.

In His directives on how the lampstand and its branches were to be fashioned, God was amazingly specific. With precise details, He painstakingly described what this light-holder was to look like. Exodus 25 is replete with definitive descriptions of *"knobs, flowers and almonds."*

Of all that lay within the universe to ornament this lampstand, God chose the fruit of a vine. His lampstand's branches would not only reflect and carry light; they were to be laden with fruit.

What sort of fruit did God select? The fruit of this lampstand, he said, *"shall be made like unto almonds"* (Exodus 25:33-34). Why almonds? *Almond*, in the Hebrew means "awakening, resurrection." The fruit of the almond tree, therefore, represents the power of new life.

In Israel, almond trees are the first to bud in the spring. They symbolize rebirth, a picture of God's ability to renew. Annually, these trees display the hope of a new day.

What does that mean to you? It means that the fruit that your God will tool into your very character carries within it the promise of being able to *"walk in newness of life"* (Romans 6:4).

Think of it, seeking Singer! Planted deep in the interior of your longing heart is a vine whose resurrection power is already coursing through you. Just like the vein of Jesus' faith discovered as you learned the song of gold, discover the seed that has power to bear fruit — *His* fruit. Resurrection is already in you.

Rejoice, Singer. You are *right now* already risen from the dead. How do I know? Because the lampstand is already singing within you.

How does this silent music, this fruit of the vine, blossom? It will flower in your responses. As the Seed within you matures, you will begin to yield your own natural reactions to frustrating people and frustrating circumstances. When you are hated, you will let Jesus love through you. When you are overwhelmed by exasperating situations, you will sing Jesus' joy. When anger arises in your spirit against someone, you will appropriate Jesus' peace. You'll be willing to put up with people, suffering the consequences of their foolishness.

There is more. Gentleness and authenticity will overtake meanness and guile. Jesus' faith will be allowed to rule your distrust of the future. You will enjoy self-control. And you will no longer feel the need to retaliate. Instead, you will agree to meekly relinquish your right to your own vigilante justice. Your false self will be silenced to let Jesus sing.

This is the fruit of the lampstand's vine:

> *But the fruit of the Spirit is love, joy, peace, longsuffering, gentleness, goodness, faith, meekness, temperance: against such there is no law.*
> Galatians 5:22-23, KJV

Know this, Singer. Fruit takes time to develop. To stand in the congregation of your church on Sunday and extravagantly sing may provide evidence that you are His branch. But when you are irritable and touchy on Monday, it proves that your fruit still needs to be ripened.

In his paraphrase of the New Testament known as The Message, Eugene Peterson writes the words of Jesus in John 4:23 this way:

> *"It's who you are and the way you live that count before God. Your worship must engage your spirit in the pursuit of truth."*

145

To grow silent singers of this caliber, much fertilizer is required. God will allow many people, situations and events to dump their refuse on you. Don't worry. Such waste material enriches the soil.

I must caution you, however. This fruit must come through God's ways and in God's time. You cannot produce your own fruit. The only fruit that you are capable of producing is fake, like plastic fruit.

You have absolutely none of the gardening skills required for this harvest. Instead, your responsibility is to yield your branch. Your willingness to be willing is the posture that's necessary.

Learn this song from the fruit-bearing branches of the lampstand: God owns everything in the universe *except* your will. That you must give.

So, when refuse is dumped on you, watch for a harvest. Yield to the circumstances that are allowed in your life. See them only as a means of cultivating the fruit seed you carry within. Trials and tribulations are the fertilizer that can yield the character of Jesus. Just surrender, *again*.

If you are willing to be willing, you will surely become what you drink from the Vine.

A Prayer at the Lampstand

Lord, I was created from You.
I was drawn from Your opened side to be Your
Bride, Your Love.
The harvest You desire is that I become the ex-
press image of our Father's nature.

The fruit that You are seeking is Your very own
character openly displayed to everyone.

Even to the cruel, the hurtful, the deliberate
hater, the thoughtless, the demander, You always
tenderly offer the opposite — Yourself.

Please, Lord, in the soil of my heart fertilize and
cultivate resurrection fruit.

For Your name's sake, I am willing to be made
willing.

And then, draw me nearer.

Chapter Fifteen

The Song of the Lamp Oil

*"And you shall command the children
of Israel that they bring you clear
oil of pressed olives for the light,
to cause the lamp to burn continually."*
(Exodus 27:20)

*T*he purpose of any lampstand is to hold a lamp. Jesus Himself said that a lamp was not to be put under a bushel, but up on a stand (see Luke 8:16).

In Moses' Tabernacle, *oil-filled lamps* were the vessels placed atop the lampstand. These containers of blazing oil pushed back the darkness. Without these lamps, the worship tent could not have known light.

> *Let your light so shine before men, that they may see your good works and glorify your Father in heaven.* Matthew 5:16

What was the catalyst for the fire? What fuel did the Creator choose to cause the lamps to burn? It was oil — pure, beaten olive oil.

In Jesus' time, olive oil was produced in one of several ways. One method involved the olive press. A huge, vertical stone wheel, pivoting on a long wooden bar, rolled over the olives and crushed them. This process was repeated until the last drops of oil were released. The oil then simply spilled into a sloping basin at the foot of the press.

The name *Gethsemane*, the place of Jesus' passion, means "oil press." The greatest test ever faced by the Son of God was in a place that was named for crushing. His agony yielded an oil of anointing and gladness that none had previously known. It is this overflow of His own oil that Jesus pours out continually within you. It is the fuel for your lamp.

There were other ways to produce oil in Jesus' time—beating and treading. Oil that is produced through beating has felt the harsh blows of men's hands. In the treading process, the oil is produced under the feet of men. Worshiper, you *will* be hurt by others. God allows it, and He will use it — if you are willing. Through such unfair treatment (of course, it is unfair) He will express His Son's oil.

So, surrender — again. In fact, sing as you are suffering these humiliations. Sing to the Lord through the crushing. By doing this, you allow the healing, glossy grace of the Holy Spirit to glide into the shattering of your false self.

In the production of olive oil, the most coveted drop of oil is called "the mother drop." This tiny drop is far purer than any other subsequent oil. It is valued beyond all other oil and is used in only the most holy anointings.

Why is this oil so coveted? It is because it is so easily extracted. This singular mother drop is most precious because it *gives up immediately*. At the *first* pressure, it surrenders. Immediate surrender is a most holy thing.

Singer, upon your journey, you have been asked to yield over and over to God. You've been asked to surrender time and time again. If you are like most singers, you wrestle with losing to God. It often takes you a while to give up. In the time before you finally give up, there can be whining, crying, bargaining or outright refusal.

The surrender song He calls you to is different. It does not hesitate. This song yields at His first touch. So, at His first touch, abandon yourself.

Every*thing*, yes, and every*one* is a tool of the Master. When you begin to really understand this truth, at His first touch you will allow the premier drop of your worship-passion to fall rejoicing into the Lord's basin. In such weakness, there is great strength:

> *I will boast all the more gladly of my weaknesses,*
> *so that the power of Christ may dwell in me.*
> 2 Corinthians 12:9, NRS

A Prayer at the Oil

*Lord, I confess that the pressures of this journey
are sometimes nearly overwhelming.
My voice trembles and cracks with dry fear even
as I pray now.*

*But I need to learn the song of unhesitating
surrender.
I need to learn to yield immediately.
I need learn to give up at Your first touch.*

*If I do, I know that the oil of anointing that
will emerge from my spirit in the process is
meant to bathe those around me with the gentleness of Jesus.*

*Allow the mother drop of my abandonment to
sing of my growing love for You.*

And draw me nearer.

Chapter Sixteen

The Song of the Holy Flame

"He shall be in charge of the lamps on the pure gold lampstand before the Lord continually."
(Leviticus 24:4)

*I*n Moses' Tabernacle, Aaron, the high priest, was to keep the lamps trimmed and burning. Their *holy flame* came from the brazen altar, where God Himself had kindled the blaze, but Aaron daily trimmed the wicks and refilled the lamps. Using golden tongs and pincers, he would remove the burned portions of the wicks. These he carefully placed into pure golden dishes to be carried outside the camp. Singer, this is how your Lord cares for the interior flame that fuels your *silent songs*.

First of all, the holy flame of Christ, deep within you, was kindled by God alone. The burning passion that you have to worship came from Jesus Himself. But the tending and fanning of this eternal fire is *also* His work. In order to intensify and glow, you are to be baptized over and over again in His fire.

The baptism of fire is an ongoing process. It is not a singular event, as you may have been taught. You need the touch of His fire daily.

If you are like most of the worshipers I know, you can easily sing of the blessings of the Lord in these days of the "positive message." One of the most popular teachings we often hear today is that we will reign with Christ. Let's look at the rest of that Scripture verse:

If we suffer, we shall also reign with him.
2 Timothy 2:12, KJV

It appears, according to this verse, that suffering precedes reigning.

At one time, I mistakenly believed that my comfort and desires were the totality of Jesus' concerns for my life. I embraced a great deception that if I worked long enough and hard enough, the Lord was obliged to visit my life with ease and simplicity. I honestly believed that my piety would insulate me against anything negative. What I came to see actualized in my life was much different. After my fervent prayers to experience the blessings of God, I was stunned by His answer. My life seemed to fall apart, as He sent His fire into it. He was responding to my cry, but in a way that was to reveal His definition of blessings, not mine.

Because of the fire in my life, I began to burn with prayer. Though at times I felt punished, even forsaken, still I cried out to know God. He was drawing me closer to Himself. Though the processes seemed cruel, to my utter amazement I began to see that in suffering and loss, I found more of Jesus. *That* was God's blessing for me.

I know now that Jesus was simply putting a blazing new song in my mouth. Over and over, the Lord allows extreme difficulties to come into our lives. And why? It is because He is the Baptizer with fire.

To baptize comes from a word that meant "to dip the wool into the dye over and over and over again." This was done to change its color. In order to reach the depth of color desired, the wool had to be dipped, or baptized, over and over in the dye. To change you, God uses the fire, and He keeps dipping you, or baptizing you, in it.

Yes, Jesus has promised us blessing, but I have found that His finest blessings are often born out of our greatest reversals. In the darkest nights of your life, He can become your finest song. In the most profound losses in your life, He can become your greatest treasure. In your deepest thirst, He can become your artesian well.

The fire is not the end, but only a means of drawing you nearer to Him. Isn't that what you have been praying for?

Look at the catalogue of silent singers in Hebrews 11. They were mocked, scandalized and ill-treated. Yet they were declared to be blessed. What was their blessing? It was that through the flames their worship grew brighter.

Does a *silent song* automatically follow the fire? No, the fire alone does not produce the music. If you still resent the process or the people God uses in the process, your song is still unsung. You will need to

159

forgive the people and embrace the process, for forgiveness is the key to this *silent song.*

Like Aaron, Jesus tenderly tends the light within you, but He must trim and renew it repeatedly. Again and again, what previously burned bright must now be cut back. Why is this continual trimming necessary? When the extraneous bulky part of the wick was removed, more flame was released. You can be streamlined by this seemingly restrictive trimming, and through the process, Jesus will be able to burn brighter within you.

As Jesus trims your lamp, He enables you to relinquish all past accomplishments. He wants you to *"forget those things which are behind"* (Philippians 3:13) so that you might press on into a new revelation ablaze with His renewed passion. He wants you to never be satisfied with being satisfied. This will require trimming your lamp.

Jesus already knows this about you, so He trims your past work and causes you to burn with new vision. In Moses' Tabernacle, Aaron's golden tongs pinched off the charred remains of yesterday's light so that new oil could flow freely again. Jesus tenderly tends your lamp. He will not extinguish even the most dimly burning wick.

Lest we become discouraged, we need to know that trimming is not the entirety of the process. Though our High Priest holds golden pincers in one hand, in His other hand is a vessel that contains soothing oil, to refresh us. Singer, when past ministries or relationships are removed from us, those burned-up wicks are immediately drowned in a new anointing of the oil of God.

Take heart. We are not to be extinguished. We are to burn for the new thing that is before us.

Silent songsters must be free — free to burn brighter in Jesus, free from the love of anything but Jesus, free from the need of anything but Jesus.

As long as the things of this world mean gain to you, your liberty, your freedom, is only an empty word, not reality. What you will gain by relinquishing is a greater treasure than what you are afraid to lose. Oh, let Him fully take hold of you, Singer!

When Christ comes to trim and remove something that we worshipers love (but which may hinder us from giving off new light), He gently comes into the Holy Place of His habitation. With His instruments of gold, He is preparing us for new passion.

We shall learn in this precise paring to sing yet another *silent song*. As we yield to His severing tool, we will find that as He cuts, He simultaneously adds multiplied intimacies of His presence—the oil of His Holy Spirit.

Blessed Singer, if the Lord comes to separate you from something you've held closely, make no mistake: He comes, not to extinguish, but to set ablaze once again.

A Prayer Before the Holy Flame

Lord, why am I afraid to be trimmed?

Is it because I am comfortable with a lukewarm flame?
Is it because it is easy to just stay where I am?

Help me to surrender those things for which I have already been passionate.
Help me to forgive the past.
Help me to exchange it for the new fire You want to grant me.

Douse me with fresh oil.
Set me ablaze anew.
Set me at liberty to sing the new song You create within me.

And then, through the flames, draw me nearer.

Chapter Seventeen

The Song of the Incense Altar

*"You shall make an altar
to burn incense on."*
(Exodus 30:1)

*W*ithin the Holy Place, standing directly in front of the veil hiding the Holy of Holies, stood a second altar—*the incense altar*. What is incense? Incense is perfumed, fragrant curls of sweet smoke rising heavenward when a substance of the same name, incense, is burned. The burning of incense produces a delightful aroma in the nostrils of God. This perfume is the song of intercession within God's holy tent.

Incense-intercession is ministry. It is Jesus' ministry:

> *He always lives to make intercession for [us.]*
> Hebrews 7:25

At this very moment, Jesus is standing before His Father on your behalf. He sings your name to the Father always. He *is* intercession.

I say this because He *is* prayer for you, and His desire is that you would become an extension of this ministry. His desire is that you would become like Him in this passionate undertaking. So, He draws you to this golden altar of prayer. This altar is the place where you will learn to sing *for others.*

165

Intercession forces abandonment of self. When your mouth is filled with the needs of others, there is no room for your own concerns. Intercession is silent music's most Christ-like melody, because this song is for someone else.

In the first Tabernacle, the altar of incense was the tallest piece of furniture. Intercession is high ministry. Surprisingly, the impact of intercession is profound both on the subject of the prayer and on the one who is doing the praying. For at this altar, the pray-*er* learns to give rather than receive. This wonderful perfume of intercession is incredibly powerful.

In Moses' time, a man named Korah led a rebellion against him. Moses did not try to manipulate anyone to save his own skin. Instead, in Christ-like fashion, he sought God's mercy for those who were betraying him. He sought benevolence, not vengeance, on his accusers by sending Aaron to stand with incense between the people and God's anger. Moses' response was silent music:

> *And Aaron took as Moses commanded, and ran into the midst of the congregation; and, behold, the plague was begun among the people: and he put on incense, and made an atonement for the people. And he stood between the dead and the living; and the plague was stayed.*
>
> Numbers 16:47-48, KJV

Oh, that the *silent song* of intercession would always be our response to accusation.

Such an aromatic melody can only be produced from the purest ingredients skillfully blended:

> *And the L*ORD *said to Moses, "Take sweet spices, stacte and onycha and galbanun, and pure frankincense with these sweet spices; there shall be equal amounts of each. You shall make of these an incense, a compound according to the art of the perfumer, salted, pure and holy. And you shall beat some of it very fine, and put some of it before the Testimony in the tabernacle of meeting where I will meet with you. It shall be most holy to you. But as for the incense which you shall make, YOU SHALL NOT MAKE IT FOR YOURSELVES, according to its composition. It shall be to you holy for the L*ORD*. Whoever makes any like it, to smell it, he shall be cut off from his people."*
> Exodus 30:34-38 (emphasis mine)

Significantly, God requires that this prayer-perfume *not* be made for our own use. It is to be made on behalf of others. Intercessory prayer is not made up of *petitions for ourselves.* This prayer is concerned with the welfare of others.

God gave specific instructions regarding the composition of the perfume. The ingredients were to be stacte, onycha, galbanum, frankincense and salt.

The first ingredient of the incense burned in the Tabernacle was *stacte*. Stacte is a gum from a tree. When any tree bleeds, its blood, or sap, is referred to as gum. Containing the very life-liquid of the tree, this gum proceeds from a pierced tree very silently and slowly. Pierced, oozing prayer is a noteworthy characteristic of worship-intercession.

The Hebrew word for *stacte* is *nataf. Nataf* has two strong meanings. First, this word means "to drip." The implication for us as worshipers is that intercession for another person is the result of being pierced by the passion of Jesus for people. And like a leaky faucet, we are to drip prayers for others persistently ... one thought, one word, one loving *drop* at a time.

The second meaning of the word *nataf* is "to distill." Distilled water is water that has been evaporated and then collected again as liquid. The result is clear, pure water that contains no parasites and no other impurities. In Third World nations, many times the existing supplies of water are unhealthful, and the result is the spread of disease. To purify unclean water requires time and money. Therefore, water that has been distilled is valuable and rare.

The implications are obvious. As we *boil* in worship-travail for others, the steamy liquid-love that is released is not only the product of much time and effort, it is also very precious in God's sight.

Onycha

The second ingredient of the perfume that arose from the altar of incense was *onycha*. Onycha was found in shellfish in the Red Sea adjacent to the wilderness of Sinai. To obtain this ingredient, the claw-shaped valves of the shellfish were removed and crushed. Only then could the onycha come forth.

These seemingly insignificant sea creatures can teach us two things about the song of intercession? First, by their very habitat, they show us that the path of deliverance for any man or woman is found through a "Red Sea" experience. Every sinner, whether family member, friend or stranger, must come out of bondage in Egypt and cross the Red Sea. You, Singer, can be the very vehicle of intercession that God uses to draw someone out of slavery and into freedom in Christ. As singers of the *silent song* of intercession, we can thus have the honor of participating in the deliverance of another.

Secondly, these shellfish were hidden in the sea. Though the water was teeming with these creatures, they were rarely, if ever, seen. Singer, with many others, you are to be a hidden vessel of intercession. Your voice, lifted in secret prayer for someone else, becomes sweet smoke at God's altar.

Galbanum

The next compound in the holy incense was *galbanum*. Galbanum has a strong, pungent and very disagreeable odor that, when used alone, aggressively drives away flies and other insects, as well as other destructive vermin.

Why add such an odious ingredient to holy incense? One of the heathen gods of ancient times was named Beelzebub, and his name literally meant "the fly-god." There were other aliases for this demon god. Among them was the distinction "the god of dung." Again, he was named this because he seemed to his worshippers to be a magnet for flies.

As you know, flies, among other insects, thrive in filth and, therefore, carry disease. This is dangerous, because they are invariably drawn to open wounds and often cause infections or something even worse.

It is not difficult to conjure up the vivid images shown on our evening newscasts of the children in war-torn, Third World countries. With no one to help them, these wounded, starving people become the targets of insidious diseases, and those diseases are often carried to them on the wings of lice, flies and other insects. These invading aggressors bring with them increased oppression and despair, and they are very real enemies of hope and restoration.

With this in mind, the implications of galbanum's use in the perfume of intercession becomes clearer. The galbanum might have been an malodorous ingredient, but it has great power to counteract the effect of filth, vermin and disease. Singer, *your* intercession, as an act of worship, has an ingredient within it that can push back every demonic oppression.

Think of it! If you (seeing the emotional, spiritual or physical wounds of others) respond in intercessory prayer, you can help drive the enemy away from them. Your intercession is a holy germicide that flushes their wounds. With the power of Jesus, your *silent song* of intercession can prevail. Any "imp" of the enemy will be driven back by this kind of selfless incense.

Frankincense

The fourth ingredient of the holy compound burned on the altar of incense was *frankincense*. Frankincense is a bitter white substance that comes from the boswellia tree. It is symbolic of fervency and passion. The gift of frankincense presented to Jesus at His nativity symbolized His passion for

His Father's will in His own life, as well His passion for those He had come to save.

Singer, when you were born again, one of the gifts brought to your nativity was the bitter, piercing passion of intercession. Worshipers are priests, priests who minister to God, priests who minister on behalf of other people.

One of our greatest failings is to respond to both of these ministries. Worship to God without love toward His Bride is incomplete. God delights to be loved, but He also wants His Wife to be loved and respected. One of the finest ways we can love one another is to pray for one another, and therefore, intercession is an act of worship.

John, in his Revelation, shows us that there are *two* parts of worship. The elders he saw standing before the throne of God had two worship articles in their hands: a harp and a bowl of incense:

And the twenty-four elders fell down before the Lamb, each having a harp, and golden bowls full of incense, which are the prayers of the saints.
Revelation 5:8

Your harp is your song of love *to* God, and your bowl of incense is your intercession *for* His people. Singer, intercession is *half* of worship. It fulfills Jesus' commandment to love your neighbor as yourself. Your willing response to the God-given

172

passion of the frankincense deposited within you is half of the bittersweet silent symphony Jesus is writing through you:

> *"You shall love the LORD your God with all your heart, with all your soul, and with all your mind. This is the first and great commandment. And the second is like it: 'You shall love your neighbor as yourself.' On these TWO commandments hang all the Law and the Prophets."*
> Matthew 22:37-39 (emphasis mine)

Frankincense is also used as a medicine and as an antidote for poison. These uses are important to us today, as well.

When you and your brother have anger or hurt feelings between you, a cancer is conceived. Cancer is a terrible, deadly disease. At first, this silent killer may go undetected. Oncologists will tell you that most cancers can be cured — if they are treated in the early stages. But because this disease is so cunning, it rarely displays any symptoms until it is very far advanced. By then, the treatment required is radical, and it may not always help.

Unresolved conflict is a cancer. Unforgiveness invades a silent singer's vital organs and does them damage. At first, your unforgiving attitude can be hidden. But eventually it betrays itself in your every word. You can't sing; you can only seethe. You are short-tempered with others. You are worn out by the grinding within your mind. Vain imaginations become constant companions. You become defensive and judgmental. And the poison of it all continues to spread. The truth is that you've laid down the cross, and you're carrying a grudge instead.

What can be done in these cases? What's the proper antidote? It is found in the ingredients of the incense: Pray for your enemies, even for those who despitefully use you, even for those who betray you, even for those who would crucify you.

Salt

The final ingredient required for making the holy incense was *salt*. Salt was extraordinarily important in biblical covenants. To the Israelites, salt was a symbol of peace, preservation and unending fidelity.

In the Bible, a "covenant of salt" is mentioned in two instances:

> *All the heave offerings of the holy things, which the children of Israel offer unto the* Lord, *have I given thee, and thy sons and thy daughters with thee, by a statue forever: it is a covenant of salt for ever before the* Lord *unto thee and to thy seed with thee.* Numbers 18:19, KJV

The Song of the Incense Altar

*Ought ye not to know that the L*ORD *God of Israel gave the kingdom over Israel to David for ever, even to him and to his sons by a covenant of salt?*
2 Chronicles 13:5, KJV

The people of the Old Testament understood the covenant of salt. To them it represented a solemn promise of utter faithfulness and dependability. For instance, if someone came to your house and ate salt at your table, an unspoken pledge of fidelity was thus established between you. The two parties were forever bound to each other in loyalty. If one of them was to commit a crime, even a capital crime, the other would not, and could not, testify against him. Any incriminating information known about that person would never be spoken aloud. They had shared salt, and the penalty for a betrayal of the intimate salt covenant was death.

A New Testament example of a broken salt covenant is revealed in Mark:

And as they sat and did eat, Jesus said, Verily, I say unto you, One of you which eateth with me shall betray me. And they began to be sorrowful, and to say unto him one by one, Is it I? and another said, Is it I? And he answered and said unto them, It is one of the twelve, that dippeth with me in the dish.   Mark 14:18-20, KJV

175

Judas, of course, was the betrayer. He had been eating the Passover with Jesus, and it included dipping "greens" into salt water. He had shared salt with Jesus, as he had done regularly for nearly three years. That same night He betrayed Jesus. It was not surprising, then, that he would take his own life when he realized what he had done. He knew that the penalty for such blatant betrayal was death.

Daily, and without fail, Singer, you eat of Jesus' salt. Daily, the covenant is confirmed as you share communion and intimacy with Him. He never leaves you, and He will never betray you. He is faithful, and His dependability is matchless. Without fail, He calls your name before the throne of His Father. Consistently, His intercession for you and for me pours forth. Although we most certainly do not deserve it, He keeps the covenant of salt. His example is our pattern.

We, the Body of Christ, have tasted the Lamb. We are in covenant with Jesus. We are also in covenant with each other, for we have shared salt. May we never be a Judas to our Lord by being a Judas to one another. Instead, let us guard one another, protecting and praying for one another, thus keeping the covenant of salt.

This means that if your brother or sister should expose any of his or her weaknesses or sins to you in strict confidence, you must never tell anyone else. The only ears that should ever hear such information should be those of Jesus. As an act of worship, you must remain silent, keeping the covenant of salt.

At the altar of incense, as we draw ever nearer to the heart of our song, let us sing its intercessory music. May our passionate prayer for others burn continually at this altar. In intercession, we join our Savior's voice at the Father's throne.

To pray for someone else is to deal another deathblow to our insatiable interest in ourselves. Such an act, though rarely visible to human eyes, is not lost to our Father's watchful gaze. He sees. To Him, the perfumed, silent music of our intercession is the sweetest of aromas.

Our worship has become the lovely fragrance of Christ.

And walk in love, as Christ also hath loved us, and hath given himself for us an offering and sacrifice to God for a sweetsmelling savor.

Ephesians 5:2, KJV

A Prayer at the Altar of Incense

*Lord, here and now in the Holy Place, I finally
hear the song of intercession.
Its notes are pure and clean.
Each selfless sound drops persistently, patiently
and powerfully into the perfume of intercessory
music.*

*Teach me the purity of that music.
Break my heart for those around me,
so that my prayer may become …*

Lord, *draw* them *nearer*.

Chapter Eighteen

The Song of Songs of the Ark

"And there I will meet with you."
(Exodus 25:22)

*T*he passion of your silent pilgrimage into the deepest chamber of interior habitation brings you to the threshold of the divine: the *Ark* of God. Singer, you stand at the very fountainhead of *silent songs.*

In the Old Testament, none dared to enter this sacred room. A thick, heavy veil separated the ordinary worshiper from the Divine Singer. Only once a year was the unseen visited, and then only by the high priest.

But not now, Singer. Because of the unspeakable gift of Christ's sacrifice, a new and living way has been cleared. Jesus, both High Priest and Veil, has torn open the way to the Father. Now, this is *your* meeting place.

Move closer, Singer. The cherubim will no longer restrain you. And because God has covered the Ark in pure mercy, you are even welcome to touch it.

The cargo of the Ark was remarkable and uncomplicated. Inside were kept the tablets inscribed with the Law, a little pot of the manna that fell miraculously each morning in the wilderness and Aaron's rod that budded. You're invited to open the Ark and know, through the simplicity of these articles, a Holy Trio: the Father, the Son and the Spirit of Holiness.

Here at the Ark you have entered into the music of the Trinity. Listen.

Throughout your journey in the wilderness, there have been no sounds, only *silent songs*. But now, in the silence, there can be heard … *something*. It is nearly imperceptible. … What is it? A rhythm? A reverberation? A voice?

Yes, it is a Voice, and each *silent song* that you have been learning was meant to help you hear *this* Voice.

In times past, you might have run away like a frightened child from an encounter such as this. But now, because you have learned in the wilderness to sing *silent songs,* your anxiety has been swallowed up by your overwhelming love for *this* Voice. This is your Shepherd. You know this voice. His perfect love has cast fear far from you.

This Voice is gently calling someone. Is that *your* name you hear?

Throughout the exploration of the Tabernacle, you thought that *you* had initiated the desire to be near this Voice. In fact, do you remember what your prayer has continually been — *Lord, draw me nearer*? Now, do you realize that it is God who has graced you with *even the desire to desire nearness*? From the outset, *He* has drawn you into hunger. *He* has helped you choose the wilderness. From the start, *He* has been whispering your name from this place in the center of your being: the tabernacle within you.

His loving song is relentless:

Child, draw near.
Child, draw near.
Child, draw near.

Even now, as He repeatedly whispers your name, He takes your hand and draws you into His waiting arms. The destination of your worship is realized in this: You are enfolded in God's embrace. In one breathless moment, you suddenly recognize the source of His voice.

His mouth has not spoken your name, His words are coming from within His breast. Grace is all you can hear. He speaks to you:

Singing child, do you understand how glad I am that you responded to My voice? Can you fathom how full of joy I am that you responded to the gift of silent music that I offered you? Can you comprehend how I delight in the fact that you freely chose Me—even in the wilderness, that, after so much losing, you haven't stopped wanting to learn to sing? This is the joy that was set before Me on the cross—you IN MY ARMS.

Oh, Singer, this is the music you will always hear now that you are leaning quietly against His heart. It is the song of the Ark that you have sought from the beginning.

Here you will be content to be alone with the Almighty. This is the song of songs.

A Prayer at the Ark

Lord, thank You for drawing me through the wilderness.
I have finally come into this quiet, most holy room.
Here at the Ark of Your presence, You have shown me that I am Your beloved child.
I am Your accepted child.

I am unspeakably thankful that You have wanted me so near to You.

Though I have lost much, I have found All.
Here, I am content to be alone with You.

I will linger here cherished upon Your breast, resting, listening to Your silence within me.

It is my song of songs.

Chapter Nineteen

Singers of Silent Songs

"I'm about to burst with song;
I can't keep quiet about you.
God, my God, I can't thank you enough."
(Psalm 30:12, MES)

ˋ

*Y*our journey from the suburbs of worship, past the city limits and into the wilderness has not been without cost. You have lost a lot. Oh, but Singer, you have gained so much! Now you're beginning to understand that all silent music is mastered through losing.

You will lose through waiting, through wrestling, through living and through dying. All of this has been accomplished to build God's holy tent of worship within you.

But, although you have lost much in the wilderness, God has won you. He has initiated and answered your prayer. He has drawn you to Himself. Beloved Singer, because of His grace you are now becoming:

- The song of surrender at His linen wall
- The praise of His colorful gate
- The shout of sacrifice at His brazen altar
- The cleansing clarity of His mirrored laver
- The embodiment of His golden pillars of faith
- The harmony within the walls of His Church
- The welcomed guest at His table of fellowship
- The expression of His unleavened bread

- The resurrection fruit of His golden lampstand
- The bearer of His fresh lamp oil
- The pray-*er* at His altar of incense

Yes, and you are the child who rests upon His breast. As you draw near to Jesus, past the ordinary into the extraordinary, He will help you to lose all that must be lost. Tenderly, He will help you relinquish it all.

If God has truly called you to learn the *silent songs* of worship, He will build within you a vestibule of Heaven that will reverberate with His own magnificent music. And He will do it in the wilderness.

Because you are to be His singer, He will expect more from you than from others who are not willing to follow Him into the desert. Other worshipers may push and manipulate in cunning ways to bring about their dreams and ministries, but you will not be allowed to.

Others may boast and be highly esteemed for their accomplishments. They may be allowed the luxury of the applause of others. You, however, may have to just sit quietly and watch as He ties your tongue and handcuffs your gifts. He may even see to it that you are not even noticed. The result may be your obscurity, but it will also be your purity.

If you allow the Maestro's tutelage, your *silent songs* will be guarded zealously by your Teacher. Every detail of His composition within you will be constantly addressed. Others may get away with being out of tune, but God will refine each note, every phrase, of your life. You will get away with nothing.

If you agree to be mentored in these *silent songs*, settle the matter with finality. Then daily, with His voice silently singing above every trial and every annoyance, draw near to Him. Listen for His words of grace minute by minute, measure by measure. Then you will know, as few have known, the miraculous silent songs of worship of God's tabernacle within you.

Can you hear Him singing? These are His words to you:

Who is this coming up out of the wilderness, leaning on her beloved?   Song of Solomon 8:5

Singer, is this you?

Ministry address:

Terri L. Terry
P.O. Box 1552
Fortson, GA 31808